Marketing Senior Housing

By Janis Ehlers

authorHOUSE®

AuthorHouse™
1663 Liberty Drive
Bloomington, IN 47403
www.authorhouse.com
Phone: 1-800-839-8640

First published by AuthorHouse 10/27/2010

ISBN: 978-1-4520-7884-7 (sc)

Printed in the United States of America

This book is printed on acid-free paper.

Acknowledgements

Thank you to the many professional friends I have made over the years who are always here for me. I greatly admire their collective talents. This second edition of **Marketing Senior Housing** would not be what it is without their help and contributions.

My first book was the result of a telephone call that every marketing-communication consultant dreams of: The National Association of Home Builder's BuilderBooks division asked me to be an author. **Marketing Senior Housing** culminated from this telephone conversation. It was a labor of love.

My gratitude is to Debbie Halsey, who has helped in so many ways to make this second edition a reality. Her editing skills polish my thoughts.

I want to thank my family and Ron Solomon. These people always believe in me and my ability to accomplish my dreams. Shirley and Ted, my mother and stepfather, are inspirational as they find joy in each day and believe their glass is full.

It is a pleasure to work with my colleague and friend, Kerry Green, who helps me so much each and every day.

Clients of my company, The Ehlers Group, provide countless opportunities to observe, absorb, and learn. The best moments come from meeting residents and hearing their stories – they give me the opportunity to walk in their shoes and see their perspectives.

When I reread my book and started rewriting the text, I was validated that many strategies still are as useful today as when I began working in the senior housing industry. My brother, Bruce Rosenblatt, always inspires me by recounting that no one sits by their telephone with their suitcases packed, awaiting a call to move to a senior community. Instead, it's the relationship that motivates a move. I hope my book inspires marketing specialists to believe in the relationship as the key to their success.

Special Cover Design Acknowledgment

My cover design was created by:

Studio Gramercy
60 Gramercy Park North
New York, New York 10019

Studio Gramercy was founded by three senior-level marketing professionals, Michael Aron, Brian Booms, and Michael Paras, with complementary talents and a shared passion for creative problem-solving. Their 25-year collaboration has furnished custom image campaigns for some of the nation's most respected companies and institutions including Ameriprise Financial, Boston Properties, U.S. Realty Advisors, and Lutheran Hospital [studiogramercy.com].

Contributors and Resources

These individuals made valuable contributions to this book:

Kristin Kutac, President, By Design Solutions, Princeton, New Jersey

Craig Smith, President, Integra Realty Resources, Sarasota, Florida

Richard G. Carlson, MIRM, CAASH, CMP, President, Carlson Communications, Northborough, Massachusetts

Mather LifeWays, Evanston, Illinois

Susan B. Brecht, President, Brecht Associates, Philadelphia, Pennsylvania

Bruce Rosenblatt, Vice President Sales, ITG Holdings, LLC, Naples, Florida

Arlene Thompson, President, Thompson Consulting, Estero, Florida

Michael Paras, Paras Photography, New York City, New York

Alaniz and Schraeder, LLP, Attorneys at Law, Houston, Texas

Table of Contents

Introduction ix

Chapter 1: New Marketing for a New Age in Senior Living 1

Chapter 2: Senior Speak for Marketing Success 5

Chapter 3: Who Is the Real Customer? – Intergenerational
            Marketing: Bridging the Family Gap 13

Chapter 4: Budgeting For Marketing Success 17

Chapter 5: Researching for Prospects and Competition 35

Chapter 6: Creating a Successful Marketing Strategy and
            Marketing Plan 47

Chapter 7: First Impressions and Setting the Stage 61

Chapter 8: Telling Your Story – From Brochures to All the
            Trimmings 71

Chapter 9: Keeping in Touch – Direct Mail and Its Use 83

Chapter 10: Advertising Strategies for Your Community 91

Chapter 11: Internet and Social Media – Evolving Marketing
            Opportunities 99

Chapter 12: Public Relations – The Most Valuable Tool 113

Chapter 13: Creative Promotional Events – A Sure Path to Prospects..133

Chapter 14: Who Leads Them to Your Door? – Spreading the Word for Referrals 149

Chapter 15: The Networking Connection – Creating and Using a Networking Plan for Outreach...............159

Chapter 16: Looking at Your Community from the Inside Out – It's All about the Customer 165

Chapter 17: The Power of Relationships 171

Chapter 18: How Are We Doing? – Monitoring and Measuring Marketing Efforts 177

Introduction

In the mid-1950s, when I was a little girl growing up in Louisville, Kentucky, I had my first experience with "care giving."

My father was an up-and-coming psychologist and my mother was an elementary school teacher. Because my mother and father both worked, my grandparents cared for me after school. Looking back, I consider myself incredibly fortunate to have received this attention from these beloved "seniors."

"... Don't ever make me live there!"

I was "Babydoll" to my grandmother (or "Mom"), for whom volunteering was a vital part of life. It was an annual ritual to play bingo on her birthday at a Jewish home for the elderly in Louisville.

One year, I joined Mom for "her day." I remember those older parents, grandparents, aunts, and uncles sitting in their wheelchairs on the front porch—most of them vacantly watching the traffic pass. I remember hoping that I wouldn't linger too long with these old and inactive people. When we finally left and climbed into my grandparents' 1953 Buick for the ride home, Mom leaned over, wagged her finger, and declared: "Babydoll, when I get really old, don't *ever* make me live there!" This was my first exposure to senior living.

After my grandfather, "Pop," passed away, my grandmother eventually moved to an apartment building. Her large house had become a burden to a lady who savored life; she wanted to be "on the go." Although her new address didn't have all of the services and amenities we now associate with many senior rental communities, it shared some of those features. For example, the affable building manager was always available to respond to residents' requests—arranging for dry cleaning pickup or mailing a package. Deliveries were a highlight; a cheerful high-schooler plunked Mom's groceries from the local A&P on her kitchen counter and laughed: "Don't want a tip!"

The building's residents enjoyed sitting in the attractive lobby in the afternoons and evenings—chatting, planning a movie outing, exchanging pleasantries and the gossip of the day, or re-hashing the *Milton Berle Show.* There was also the security and peace of mind that comes with living with others like yourself—others you cared about and who cared about you.

This was, in a sense, the precursor of today's independent living or senior rental community—without the communal dining room and recreational amenities, but with the all-important camaraderie of being with your contemporaries.

Perception vs. Reality

How far we've come. The stereotypical, anonymous "old folks' home" of the first half of the 20th century has given way to a wide range of senior housing options from assisted living to "lifestyle" communities tailored to the tastes and requirements of specific senior populations. Today, senior communities and definitions of "senior housing" are as varied as our choices in vehicles.

In the following chapters, you'll find a wealth of proven tools, techniques, and "nontraditional" strategies that will help you succeed in marketing the new and still-evolving paradigm of senior housing.

Chapter 1:

|||||||||||||||||||||||||||||||||||||||||||||||||||||||||||||||||||||||||||||||||||||||||||||||||||||||||||||||||

New Marketing for a New Age in Senior Living

To begin, it's important to understand the varied industry definitions incorporated in the term "senior housing." They include assisted living facilities (ALF), continuing care retirement communities (CCRC), and independent living communities (IL). You should also understand what each type offers and the various financial plans commonly associated with each. Each type of community is unique, with its own advantages and drawbacks.

To make these classifications more generic to the industry, organizations such as the American Association of Homes & Services for the Aging (AAHSA), American Health Care Association (AHCA), American Seniors Housing Association (ASHA), Assisted Living Federation of America (ALFA), National Center of Assisted Living (NCAL), National Investment Center for the Seniors Housing & Care Industry, Inc. (NIC), and National Association of Home Builders (NAHB) 50+ Housing Council have endorsed these as standard definitions:

Active Adult Communities – For-sale single family homes, town homes, cluster homes, mobile homes, and condominiums with no specialized services, restricted to adults at least 55 years of age or older. Rental housing is not included in this category. Residents generally lead an independent lifestyle; communities are not equipped to provide increased care as the individual ages. Communities may include amenities such as clubhouses, golf courses, and recreational spaces. Outdoor maintenance is normally included in the monthly homeowners' association or condominium fee.

1

Senior Apartments – Multifamily, residential rental properties restricted to adults at least 55 years of age or older. These properties do not have central kitchen facilities and generally do not provide meals to residents, but may offer community rooms, social activities, and other amenities.

Independent Living Communities – Age-restricted, multifamily rental properties with central dining facilities that provide residents, as part of their monthly fee, access to meals and other services such as housekeeping, linen service, transportation, and social and recreational activities. Such properties do not provide, in a majority of the units, assistance with activities of daily living (ADLs) such as supervision of medications, bathing, dressing, toileting, and so on. There are no licensed skilled nursing beds on the property.

Assisted Living Residences, also known as Assisted Living Facilities – State-regulated rental properties that provide the same services as independent living communities listed above, but also provide, in a majority of the units, supportive care from trained employees for residents who are unable to live independently and require assistance with ADLs including management of medications, bathing, dressing, toileting, ambulating, and eating. These properties may have some nursing beds, but the majority of units are licensed for assisted living. Many of these properties include wings or floors dedicated to residents with Alzheimer's disease or other forms of dementia. A property that specializes in the care of residents with Alzheimer's or other forms of dementia, that is not a licensed nursing facility, should be considered an assisted living property.

Nursing Homes – Licensed daily rate or rental properties that are technically referred to as skilled nursing facilities (SNF) or nursing facilities (NF), where the majority of individuals require 24-hour nursing and/or medical care. In most cases, these properties are licensed for Medicaid and/or Medicare reimbursement. These properties may include a minority of assisted living and/or Alzheimer's/dementia units.

CCRCs – Age-restricted properties that include a combination of independent living, assisted living, and skilled nursing services (or independent living and skilled nursing) available to residents, all on one campus. Resident payment plans vary and include entrance fee, condo/coop, and rental programs. The majority of the units are not licensed skilled nursing beds.

Those embarking on careers in senior housing, as well as in the development of senior-focused communities, should acquaint themselves thoroughly with these different types of communities and the nuances of each as well as how each is regulated. Varying state laws, for example, define nomenclature for assisted living as a basis for meeting licensing requirements (for example, what separates a "nursing home" from a "nursing facility").

Also, the industry is evolving and what may be the definition today may change based on the growing adaptability of the marketplace. For example, in Florida, a continuing care community implies a financial plan for a resident, not a rental plan. In Georgia, an owner referred to his rental community, which offered independent, assisted, and skilled nursing living residences, as a continuing care community. Figuring out the nomenclature is not only difficult for marketers of senior housing, but for consumers, as well. Consult state statutes to make sure you are referring to your community by its correct name.

Today, we're redefining senior markets and retooling marketing philosophies. Senior demographics are rapidly changing as the "Boomer" generation enters retirement age, and their expectations for housing represent a sea change from traditional concepts.

We're also recognizing that seniors are not a monolithic population that we can lump together as "the elderly." Thanks to advances in healthcare, increased longevity, lifelong learning programs, and fast-evolving definitions of what "being old" means, there are distinct and varied populations of seniors with communities that "fit" their level of independence, physical needs, and lifestyle expectations.

The problem? For many, outdated perceptions of "the elderly" and "old folks' homes" refuse to disappear. The challenge for senior housing marketing professionals is to change those perceptions.

Common Thread: Caring

No matter what its stripe, the success of any single senior community will be determined by the sincerity and sustaining attitude that comes with one all-important word: caring.

The presence or absence of a tangible and consistent attitude of caring percolates down throughout a community, from top management to nursing aides, maintenance staff, and dining room servers. It can make or break any given community, no matter how impressive the physical plant or tasteful the decor or landscaping.

The old folks' home of years gone by, which in some cases was justifiably regarded as a warehouse for the elderly ("God's waiting room"), was based on an antiquated, custodial concept of "care." Modern senior housing communities reflect a new and enlightened concept of what care for seniors can and should be.

Senior housing has truly come a long way, and marketing professionals have a range of senior community "products" to offer. Our marketing challenge is twofold: battling old myths about housing for seniors, and effectively promoting the new, caring face of today's senior housing industry.

Chapter 2:

||||||||||||||||||||||||||||||||||||||||||||||||||||||||||||||||||||||||||||||||||||||||||||||||||||||

Senior Speak for Marketing Success

Especially when marketing senior communities, choose your words carefully. The language to communicate to seniors is critical to your success and deserves special consideration during all aspects of marketing, as well as when practiced by your community's staff.

Basic terminology associated with senior communities is somewhat confusing and easily misunderstood by the consumer. Unless they have been personally involved with a senior community, the media, referral sources, adult children of potential residents, and even future residents many times do not understand the nuances among the various community options and within the industry language.

The differences between independent and assisted living versus a continuing care community may seem basic to those of us in the profession, but they are not obvious to the consumer. An interested salesperson asking if "Mom needs assisted living" may draw a blank stare from the adult child who really doesn't know what Mom needs.

"Senior speak" is terminology geared to the specialized senior housing market—a vocabulary that respects seniors and understands the hot buttons that can either reassure and draw them in, or send them on to the next community. Think about it: would you rather move to a "unit" in a "facility" or to a "residence" in a "community"?

As prospective residents narrow their choices in senior communities, they and their family members are receptive to marketing materials and messages that are well expressed and genuinely informative. In addition, using the right words creates a trickle-down benefit as your management and staff mirror your own vocabulary.

Remember that:
- It is often the subliminal messages that attract or repel prospective residents and their families.
- The focus must always be on dignity.

Why Is It So Confusing?

An initial source of confusion is in the word "senior." The thesaurus offers a variety of alternatives including "old person," "elderly," "curmudgeon," and "octogenarian." But "senior" may simply imply an adult or someone of an advanced age, especially at or past retirement. To further the confusion, some may consider "senior" a compliment (as in, a "senior partner"), while others may find it a negative.

The term "senior citizen discount" is not defined consistently by a chronological age. For every movie theater offering a discount for someone age 60+, there is a retail store offering a discount for those age 55+. But are these folks really seniors when the U.S.'s new retirement age is 67? People age 55+ consider "seniors" their parents—not themselves!

People tend to think of themselves as 20 years younger than their chronological age. If you ask a senior housing developer/owner the age of his or her audience, it gets tricky. As they try to label their audiences, they tend to use unqualifying age words such as "active adults," "older adults," "matures," and "seniors." But residents vary in their age and abilities.

There are those of us who believe age is simply a number and doesn't indicate where you want to live now or into the future. There are 80-year-olds still desiring to live in a single family home, caring for the house and handling all of its responsibilities, while there are other 80-year-olds desiring more services and lifestyle amenities, and planning for their later years.

In the field of senior housing, we reach two audiences that may both technically be seniors: the adult children may be in their 60's while their parents are in their 80's. Both need marketing language that they will perceive as professional, helpful, caring, and upbeat.

Expressions and Vocabulary to Lose

Many of us who enter the senior housing industry may bring with us the vocabulary of either real estate or healthcare. But often these words may be inappropriate when applied to today's senior housing consumer. A few common words and terms can send the wrong messages when marketing senior communities.

Units

To a developer/owner, "units" means the number of residential apartments or houses in a given development. To a physician or nurse, a "unit" is a type of measurement. To most senior consumers, the term is unappealing and doesn't speak to their emotions. Remember, you are leasing or selling homes and residences—not units.

Facility

"Facility" conveys, directly or subliminally, a similarly depressing, custodial/medical/institutional message. We are motivated by a subliminal message of home and hearth. While the senior care industry may use the term in describing an independent, assisted living, or skilled care residence, you should banish the word "facility" from marketing collateral and everyone's vocabulary. "Community" is a much-preferred alternative and people live in communities—not facilities.

Artist's Rendering

During a tour, it may be useful to show a prospective resident the preliminary drawings of the community. In these cases, it may be more understandable to the consumer to use the term "artist's interpretation" or "artwork" rather than "rendering"—which conjures the image of a vat of fat.

Topo Table

Better to refer to this as the "scale model," as in "Let me show you our scale model to give you a better idea of where you are in relation to where your apartment will be when you move to (community name)."

"Topo" is a real estate expression for "topographical" and may meet with a blank stare from the customer.

Leasing, Sales, and Information Centers

This is a no-brainer. "Welcome Center" is so much more...welcoming! Depending on your market, you may want to consider some of the newest terms such as "Discovery Center." But you can never go wrong with "Welcome Center," which sends a message of a warm welcome and feeling of hospitality.

A visitor (an 80-year-old man) walks in to the Sales Center of a senior housing community. He is greeted by a "sales counselor"— that is what they usually call salespeople who work in senior housing. Young people are quite up to dealing with salespeople; however, being old is commonly perceived as such as handicap of body and mind that the humane thing to do is to repackage the same salesperson as a "sales counselor" before he or she is permitted to go into the sales arena with an "old person." Old people need counseling: young people, despite considerably less experience in buying, don't. (*Marketing to Boomers and Beyond: Strategies for Reaching America's Wealthiest Market*, David B. Wolfe)

Overblown Staff Titles

Staff titles in the Marketing Department may run the gamut from "leasing rental counselors" to "lifestyle counselors," "leasing agents," "retirement counselors," and "marketing representatives," to name a few. Call different communities to learn what titles they are using. Designating the leasing staff at your community as "salespeople" is not negative since, after all, their responsibility is to sell.

Impersonal Pronouns

You may have noticed that physicians and psychologists seldom use pronouns when referring to family members. "Mom" and "Dad" are warmer and more personal than "your mother" and "your father." They are also less risky since customers may be in-laws rather than parents.

Whether or not Mom and Dad are present, never refer to them as "he" or "she" as if they were small children (as in "How do you think he would feel about moving here?"). Remember, we don't "move Mom and Dad to a home"; we help them with their decision to select a residence that is the right choice for their lifestyle.

Presumed Informality

Your customer has earned respect and should be referred to as Mr., Mrs., or Ms. He or she may instruct you otherwise but, in deference to etiquette, it is advisable to continue to be more formal. What begins at Leasing may trickle down to other staff, and practicing this respect is a small touch that is appreciated.

"Three Meals a Day"

This phrase is much less appealing than "Our dining room serves breakfast, lunch, and dinner at these times...." If you can insert some appetizing adjectives to further describe your community's nutritious and savory menu items, so much the better!

Unfamiliar Language

Don't use industry-shortened terms (like IL, AL, ALF, CCRC, and SNF) when conversing with customers. They really do not know these acronyms. Instead, draw on the vocabulary familiar to your customers and your specific locale. For example, those of us from Florida might not relate to a "country kitchen" but we are comfortable with references to an "outdoor kitchen" or "lanai."

More Great Vocabulary	
Consider Using:	Instead of:
Director of First Impressions	Receptionist or Hostess
Lifestyle Coordinator or Entertainment Director	Activity Director

Director of Building Services	Director of Maintenance
Food and Beverage Director	Dining Room Manager
Chef	Cook
Transportation Specialist	Bus Driver
Residents	Patients
Club Members (if applicable)	Residents
Lifestyle Community	Senior Community
Neighborhood	Project
Technology Center	Computer Room
Village Store	Convenience Store

"A Room of One's Own"

When you are thinking of names for community amenities and areas, think about world-class hotels and cruise ships. In both industries, creating a favorable guest experience is practiced on a daily basis and tremendous thought is placed on the naming of amenities for critical impact.

"Multipurpose Room" or "Community Room" doesn't sound nearly as inviting as "Party Room" or "Living Room." Similarly, "Arts Studio" is infinitely more appealing than "Arts and Crafts Room." You will find "Spa" more attractive than "Workout Room" and "Health Club" or "Fitness Studio" more enticing than "Gym." "Communication Center" may take the place of "Computer Room" or "Mail Room."

When making these choices, however, don't be too "cutesy" or "cheesy." To your future residents, the community is a potential home and it's important to use words that conjure home-like livability.

Language and Signage

Words set a tone and ambiance, and they can free us from the stereotypes associated with aging. This may start from the impression made by the community's entry signage. Here the copy used on the exterior signage is crucial.

Entry signs are not advertisements and are not intended to tell the community's story. It is not necessary to clutter your exterior sign with copy that explains what you are. Most customers are not driving up and down city streets shopping for a community. More than likely they have made an appointment and are driving directly to your location. What they are looking for is your sign to confirm their arrival at the right place. Descriptive tag lines on signs (such as "an assisted living community") are unnecessary and may stereotype your community as the "old folks' home" in the neighborhood.

It also is not necessary for the exterior signage to provide a telephone number. Instead, an attractive monument sign should provide the community name.

A temporary sign can offer more information and is used, when needed, for pre-leasing, tours, and so on. It may offer enough information that someone who is interested may either inquire by calling or visiting a web site to schedule a tour.

Chapter 3:

IIIIIIIIIIIIIIIIIIIIIIIIIIIIIIIIIIIIIIIIIIIIIIIIIIIIIIIIIIIIIIIIIIIIIIIIIIIIIIIIIIIIIIIIIIIIIIIIIIIIIIIIIIIIIIIIIIIIIIIIIIIIIIIIII

Who Is the Real Customer? – Intergenerational Marketing: Bridging the Family Gap

When it comes to marketing senior housing, it's not always clear who the real customer may be. Ultimately we know the resident's profile, but the prospect and initial inquiry source may not be the prospective resident. Determining the influencers and the real decision makers can be a challenge for a salesperson and for a successful marketing program.

In Naples, Florida, a husband and wife in their early 60's are enjoying an active, country club lifestyle. The wife's elderly mother lives in suburban Chicago and suffers from macular degeneration. This daughter feels that having her mother live with her and her husband would not work, but she is naturally concerned about her mother's decreasing ability to get around, shop, bank, visit doctors, and so on. The daughter visits a Naples luxury, senior community as a potential customer to gather information. Later that winter, her mother comes to Naples to visit the family and also visits the senior community. Both mother and daughter will surface in databases as customers, but only the mother is a prospective resident.

"You Just Don't Understand"

What parent of a typical teenager hasn't heard this wail of frustration? Often this same kind of generational disconnect can occur in your sales office. You need to be prepared to speak to multiple generations. Assume that Mom and Dad, accompanied by their son, have just arrived for a tour. Your primary customers—the parents—are both age 80+. The son—your secondary customer—is 60+ and you are 37. How do you bridge these generation gaps and effectively communicate with these prospects while drawing on your own frame of reference and values?

The excellent book *Rocking the Ages: The Yankelovich Report on Generational Marketing* (J. Walker Smith and Ann S. Clurman), refers to generations as Matures, Boomers, and Xers. The situation described above includes the combination of Matures (born between 1909 and 1945), Boomers (born between 1946 and 1964), and Xers (born between 1965 and 1976). Most likely this will be typical of the majority of your Welcome Center scenarios.

Our primary customers are Matures, whose core values were shaped from growing up during the Depression and World War II, and living through the Cold War era. These people typically have worked hard, scrimped, and saved their money. They tend to believe retirement and leisure time are rewards for hard work.

Our customer's child is of the Boomer generation. Stereotypes of the Boomer generation include a sense of entitlement and a tendency to be self-absorbed and consumed with personal goals, self improvement, and instant gratification.

Beware of these stereotypes. No individual *is* his or her generation and some people change dramatically as they age, whereas others evolve less or remain essentially the same. So don't assume that any prospect is an exact stereotype of his or her generation; instead, be perceptive. You can often tell more about an individual from clues gleaned in 10 minutes of targeted conversation than from assumptions about generational stereotypes.

However, certain mindsets and beliefs are prevalent to each generation and it can be helpful to understand them. Typical Boomers may look in disbelief at their parents' desire to live simply, quietly, and securely among their contemporaries. Yet that environment is exactly what many members of the Matures generation find most desirable and comforting. Most Matures rank crime and personal safety among their chief concerns. For these people, gated, secure retirement communities offer refuge from the outside world.

Matures also seek value—reassurance that their money is well spent—because their generation values frugality and responsibility and is fiscally cautious.

Boomers are often preoccupied with how stressful their lives are and seek relief from stress. Having Mom and Dad happily and independently ensconced in a secure retirement community can be a way of mitigating their own stress level.

The Boomer children sitting across from you who are helping Mom and Dad with their decision may be interested in the activity programs your community offers and convinced that self-improvement (exercise programs, educational seminars, art classes, and so on) are essential to their parents' happiness. This may not be so. It is important to talk to both generations and trust your instincts about who will ultimately make the decision.

Many Boomers are nonconformists and doubting by nature. They may be encouraging Mom and Dad to do strategic shopping of senior communities before making the decision. Reassurance is key. It is important to stress to these children that your community is not cookie-cutter in its programs and that it provides flexibility and conveniences. If you sense the parents are enthusiastic about your community but deterred by their children, it may be worthwhile to encourage them to visit the competition to see for themselves your community's strengths.

The key word is "discovery." We are entering the new world of relationship marketing and you are called upon to blend the skills of counseling with selling.

Chapter 4:

||||||||||||||||||||||||||||||||||||||||||||||||||||||||||||||||||||||||||||||||||||||||||||||||||||||||||||

Budgeting For Marketing Success

The developer/owner who asks "So, how much will this cost?" is really asking "What's the least I have to spend?" The consultant may respond "So, what's your budget?" and what he or she is trying to determine is how much the developer/owner is willing to spend.

This is a challenge right from the start—determining how much must be spent to be successful. When launching a community, the decision requires the experience of others to say how much is needed. Spending money *well* is key. You are seeking a budget that allows for creativity and will sustain marketing efforts over the course of time.

The mere mention of the word "budget" can make many "creative types" cringe. Fear not because creating a marketing budget really isn't rocket science. A budget is just numbers and spreadsheets. User-friendly accounting software can automate much of the process. These programs are also adept at "what if" projections and can crunch numbers easily to show variables.

Like it or not, adhering to a well-thought-out budget is fundamental to a successful marketing program. The ability to strategically project marketing expenses needed to bring traffic to the door and convert visitors to customers is a skill honed by experience.

A budget is an essential tool that helps you allocate resources efficiently, a reality check that keeps you on target, and a buffer against nasty surprises (like spending dollars to successfully bring traffic to your community's door and then finding you have little left to convert that traffic to sales/leases with a grand opening, or nothing set aside to reorder brochures).

From community to community, marketing budgets vary widely in both expenditures and dollar allocations. Each may have different ways of categorizing and prioritizing expenses. For example, larger communities, which may use outside agencies for research, advertising placement, and other marketing functions, may not itemize individual service areas if included within the overall agency fee.

Your first budget will be the most difficult to develop, but it will be well worth the effort. It's a road map that helps you track where you've been, where you need to go, and how much gas (money) you have left to get there. It helps you determine if your marketing program's goals are realistic and within reach. You will start developing a history of knowing what it costs to create sales.

In essence, an initial budget is a detailed plan of future expenditures. Some budgets may also project expenditures against projected sales. In other words, if you spend "x," how many deals will you close (for example, how many apartments will you lease)? *Tip:* This is the most challenging budgeting concept to grasp, but can be done by: 1) projecting the realistic number of sales needed (industry standards can help provide the realistic number of deals that can be done per month); 2) backing into the expenditures; and 3) dividing total expenditures by the number of sales.

A budget is part of the marketing plan. (It translates the marketing plan into numbers through a "chart of accounts.") In creating a budget that is realistic, it is important to determine how much money is needed to survive, maintain your image, and, if necessary, expand your reach.

We had a client who believed in a blitz marketing approach to launch a new senior community. They sought to go all-out with full-page advertising, direct mail to targeted zip codes, special events, and publicity. When it came to budgets, there were no holds barred. While their competitors were using frequent, small-space ads, this launch was dramatic. With marketing budgets untypical to the senior housing industry, their effort to set the community apart from competition certainly worked. The buzz was significant and everyone in town knew the community's name and was eager for the doors to open. An added benefit for the new community: prospective employees were eager to apply for positions.

The challenge many communities encounter is believing that, because they are occupied and/or have waiting lists, they do not need to advertise, use publicity, or spend additional marketing dollars. This is hardly the truth. Cutting back the marketing budget has far-reaching ramifications. Once the noise stops, so does the community's marketing momentum. When the community becomes less known by new prospects entering the marketplace, referral sources stop thinking of the community. An aggressive budget may be needed to restart the cycle again.

Remember, everyone's marketing scenario will be different, and your budget should reflect your resources, priorities, and challenges.

Budget Smart – Spend Money Well

Decide early on what should or can be included in (or excluded from) your marketing budget. Take exterior signage, for example. You need signage to open the community, and may assume that this cost would come out of your direct marketing budget. But if you're strategic, creative costs for the logo design would hit the marketing budget while the signage itself, which is permanent, would find its way into the building's fixture budget. Down the road, repainting the signage would be an operations cost rather than marketing cost—though it certainly is a marketing issue if repainting is needed. Whew!

Here's one rule of thumb: *If the primary purpose of an item is to attract and convert prospects to sales or leases, it probably should be treated as a direct marketing expense.*

When drawing up your initial marketing plan, consider questions and issues such as the following when projecting costs:

- Community size – How many apartments need to be leased?
- Timing – Does this start-up community need pre-leasing? Does an existing community needing a repositioning program?
- Maintaining census – If apartments are currently 98% leased, how do you maintain the census?
- Staffing – Are leasing teams' salaries and commissions part of the marketing budget in terms of dedicated positions? Or are these positions budgeted in operations?
- Marketing versus operations – If you utilize the dining room

for providing refreshments or the activity director for planning events to generate traffic, will you allocate these related costs to the marketing budget or charge the operations budget?

When we were asked to develop a marketing budget for a new project, my associate, Claire, was overwhelmed at the prospect. "How do I know if or when I'll need a sales brochure reorder?" she wondered. Well, maybe the brochures will last through the year, and maybe they won't. Here the better-safe-than-sorry rule applies: when in doubt, project the expenditure. Sure, you can take the money from another category, but better to budget for it initially and then show unspent funds.

There was more confusion in how to treat actual versus budgeted expenditures. Claire felt that, if she had budgeted $100 in a given month for classified ads but spent $200, she should enter only $100—the budgeted amount—for that month and move the excess $100 into the next month. Bad practice. Indicate the actual $200 spent and know that there was a variance of $100 for that month.

Figure 4-1. Checklist budget for start-up community marketing.

I. Sales Office/Model Expenses (temporary structure)

Maintenance	_____
Utilities	_____
Telephone/fax/Internet access	_____
Real estate taxes	_____
Unit interest and/or rental	_____
Furnishings and fixtures (including depreciation)	_____
Equipment	_____
Interior/exterior finishing	_____

Landscaping/awning/
detailing   _____

Signage (permitting, de-
sign, fabrication, installa-   _____
tion and maintenance)

II. Sales Salaries

Base salaries and/or   _____
commissions

Bonuses   _____

Clerical support - staff   _____
salaries

Broker compensation   _____

Training   _____

Recruitment   _____

Allowances (travel, enter-   _____
tainment, etc.)

Miscellaneous (welcome   _____
gifts, flowers, decorations)

III. Merchandising

Logo design/sales displays   _____

Display and exhibit design   _____
and fabrication

Scale model fabrication   _____

Pre-sales collateral (preview   _____
brochure, mail-outs, etc.)

Permanent collateral pack-   _____
age (brochure, renderings,
floor plans, pricing, site
plan)

Sales forms   _____

Stationery package   _____

Model apartment décor and   _____
furnishings

Welcome Center décor and   _____
furnishings

IV. Media Advertising (local, regional, national)
    Agency retainer and/or
    project fee   _____

    Media planning and
    placement   _____

    Print and production (con-
    cept/layout, cooperative
    ads)   _____

    Photography   _____

    TV/radio advertising
    (concept/storyboard,
    production)   _____

    Miscellaneous expenses   _____

V. Public Relations/Community Relations
    Agency retainer and/or
    project fee   _____

    Media planning and
    placement   _____

    Print and production (con-
    cept/layout, cooperative
    ads)   _____

    Photography   _____

    TV/radio advertising
    (concept/storyboard,
    production)   _____

    Miscellaneous expenses   _____

V. Public Relations/Community Relations
    Agency retainer and/or
    project fee   _____

    Press releases (copywriting,
    photography, distribution)   _____

    Promotions and spe-
    cial events (cost out
    individually)   _____

    Event planning   _____

Community awareness
programs _____

Pre-sales Open House
programs _____

Community relations (on-
going resource contacts) _____

Participation in charity and
community-oriented events _____

Special budget: Direct mail (copywriting, creative design,
printing, distribution)

Special budget: Marketing newsletters (design and layout,
copywriting, photography, printing, distribution)

Special budget: Community newsletter (same items as above)

VI. Miscellaneous

Other compensations ("shared" sales commissions/bonuses,
supervisory salaries, management company fees, legal fees,
conventions, meetings attendance)

Marketing research (agency/consultant fees)

Corporate public relations (for developer/owner, tied to
project)

Collateral additions (package inserts, special items such as
resident move-in booklet, community services such as activity
calendar)

Promotional give-aways (logo'ed coffee mugs, t-shirts, etc.)

Special projects (contingency for unplanned programming)

Other special costs

Parable of the Logo and Spending Money Well

Prioritize your marketing expenditures based on the time-honored "most-bang-for-the-buck" principle. Don't stint where a big or lasting pay-off is likely. Take the one-time expense of community logo design, for example. This all-important, branding identity will appear on everything from the front entry awning to ads and collateral, coffee mugs, letterhead, and web sites for years to come.

Sure, you can design a community logo on your own computer. Perhaps the printer who does your business cards will offer to design one for you. You may find a graphic designer who doesn't take the time to get a clear focus on your specific community while another person does. Some logos will be undistinguishable; some will be OK; and some will be memorable and award-winning—enduring the test of time and reflecting the essence of the community and the corporation of which it is a part. So, logo design can range from $50 to thousands of dollars. Is paying more worth it? Probably.

Before you budget, it goes without saying that you should have an in-depth understanding of your community, its niche, and the image your community wants to project as its brand. For example, a community with church sponsorship may need to show a different image from a continuing care community seeking a larger financial commitment from a potential resident.

Be aware that budgets are not written in stone; they must be flexible enough to accommodate shifting market conditions and strategic reallocations of funds. For example, you may decide that your client would be better served by redirecting money budgeted for advertising to a targeted E-blast or direct mail campaign.

Inevitably, you'll find there are expense categories you've overlooked or didn't anticipate that should be in your chart of accounts. It's common for budgets for a given community to become more fine-tuned as time goes on.

Budget Timing

Budget timing normally parallels the development/occupancy path. Because most projects involve at least a year's time for build-out, expenses will normally need to be fixed within the same time period.

In communities financed with construction and then permanent loans, funds are usually drawn by the developer/owner at pre-designated intervals with specific costs assigned within each phase of construction. You will need to know when these draws occur to keep marketing costs timed to (and within the limits of) available funding.

Key areas which entail budgeting for marketing purposes:

- Conceptual planning to pre-occupancy/sales – Announcement of the community, opening of Welcome Center, launch of marketing programs to generate deposits/pre-occupancy lease-up, and retention of these early depositors
- Conversion to first occupancies – Conversion of first depositors to residents with Grand Opening follow-up, first resident move-ins, first resident activities/services, conversion of visitor tours, nearing close of available residences in first phase
- Maintenance – On-going efforts to maintain occupancy goals including on-going promotions and communication to lead base, continually generating new traffic

While budgeting can start at any time, it's normally more efficient to tie the process to the fiscal year of your client. That way you'll be "in sync" with the budgetary cycle. Annualized budgeting can be phased in to track fiscal year financing, including a full year of operations following the lease-up or sales periods. This type of budget is normally developed to maintain a projected occupancy rate (typically 90%+), and will include such items as continuing communications, traffic-building events, and costs similar to those incurred during first-phase leasing and maintenance of projected occupancies going forward.

Where do staffing costs fit in? Good question. Costs for an individual or staff responsible only for sales may be carried either within the community's administrative budget as salary expense, or assigned directly to the marketing budget. Methods of sales payments, especially for draw and commission plans with bonus and incentive provisions, vary among different communities depending on the ongoing sales or leasing plans.

Where Am I?

It's a no-brainer, but when the pace is frenetic it's easy to forget: take the time to continually review and evaluate your budget so that you know where you are and how you're doing against plan. If you don't regularly track outflows against balances, you can wake up one day and realize that you have no money left for promoting that crucial open house planned for the end of the year.

Budget "Buckets"

You should set up pre-determined cost categories accounting for every marketing expenditure and the anticipated time of the expense. While budget organization varies among communities, almost all marketing costs exist within some common, major categories. Answers to these three basic questions can help direct detailed categorization:

- What is the specific expense?
- When will it be used?
- How much will it cost?

Typically, there are six major categories in a typical senior community marketing budget, with various sub categories:

- Advertising
- Direct mail
- Merchandising
- Sales
- Public relations
- Miscellaneous

Figure 4-2. Sample community marketing budget.

DESCRIPTION	JAN	FEB	MAR	APR	MAY	JUN	JUL	AUG	SEP	OCT	NOV	DEC	TOTAL
ADVERTISING:													
Linage													0
Production													0
Internet Ads													0
Radio - airtime													0
Radio - production													0
BROCHURES & INSERTS:													
Printing													0
Production													0
DIRECT MAIL:													
Production & Printing													0
Postage													0
KIOSK:													
Production													0
Space													0

SAMPLE BUDGET

NEWSLETTERS:										
Production & Printing	0									
Postage	0									
PHOTOGRAPHY:										
Aerial	0									
Lifestyle	0									
Stock	0									
Model Photos	0									
SALE CENTER DISPLAYS:	0									
MARKETING SERVICES:	0									
COMMUNITY RELATIONS:	0									
SIGNS & BANNERS:	0									

SPECIAL EVENTS (including brokers):												0
STATIONERY & FORMS:												0
VIDEO:												
Production – update												0
Duplication												0
WEB SITE:												
Design & Production												0
E-mail Blasts												0
Hosting & Maintenance												0
TOTALS:	$0	$0	$0	$0	$0	$0	$0	$0	$0	$0	$0	$0

Source: Carlson Communications, Richard G. Carlson, President

How these categories break down will differ in a start-up versus a one-year budget.

A start-up budget will be your most expensive, because it assumes you are starting a community from ground zero. When developing this budget, it is often cost efficient to turn to specialized consultants and resources for the realistic numbers they can project based on their experience and expertise. *Tip:* If your ad agency knows they are your agency, they are far more receptive to helping you with this exercise!

The following list assumes a full-blown start-up. A one-year-old community marketing program or a program mix for a repositioning would probably not entail all of these expenses.

Figure 4-3. Major categories in a comunity marketing budget.

Advertising
✓ Identity _____
  – Community naming _____
  – Branding image _____
  – Tagline_____
  – Logo_____
✓ Stationary package (letterhead, envelopes, business cards, labels) _____
  – Design _____
  – Printing _____
✓ Collateral _____
  – Brochure package_____
  – Design and copywriting _____
  – Artwork (renderings, other) _____
  – Printing _____
  – Brochure smaller version_____
  – Printing _____
✓ Photography_____
  – Photo shoots interior/exterior _____
  – Models _____
  – Props, creative director, stylists_____
  – Royalty-free stock images _____

✓ E-communication _____
   – Web site _____
   – Design _____
   – Copywriting_____
   – E-blasts and E-postcards _____
   – E-newsletter _____
   – Search engine media plan_____
   – Social media plan _____
✓ Print advertising_____
   – Newspaper ads _____
   – Magazine ads _____
   – Event ad design _____
   – Yellow Page advertising _____
   – Charity ads _____
✓ Media planning and strategy _____
✓ Agency retainer _____

Direct Mail
✓ Postcard campaign _____
   – Fulfillment _____
   – Postage_____
✓ Invitations _____
✓ Flyers _____

Merchandising
✓ Sales office/model expenses_____
   – Maintenance _____
   – Utilities _____
   – Telephone/fax/Internet access_____
   – Rental of office space/trailer _____
   – Furnishings and fixtures (including depreciation) _____
   – Equipment (computers, HD TVs, telephones, coffee machine) _____
   – Displays and exhibits (virtual tours) _____
   – Interior/exterior finishing _____
   – Landscaping/awning/detailing _____

- Signage (permitting, design, fabrication, installation, and maintenance) _____
- Scale model fabrication_____
- Model apartment décor (furniture, fixtures, and special upgrades) _____
- Welcome Center décor (furniture, fixtures, and special features) _____

Sales
- ✓ Base salaries and/or commissions _____
- ✓ Bonuses _____
- ✓ Clerical support – staff salaries _____
- ✓ Referral compensation _____
- ✓ Training_____
- ✓ Recruitment _____
- ✓ Allowances (travel, entertainment, and so on)_____
- ✓ Miscellaneous (welcome gifts, flowers, decorations) _____
- ✓ Sales contracts and business cards_____

Public Relations and Community Relations
- ✓ Press releases (copywriting, photography, distribution) _____
- ✓ Promotions and special events (cost out individually) _____
- ✓ Community awareness programs _____
- ✓ Event planning_____
- ✓ Pre-sales events_____
- ✓ Community relations (ongoing resource contacts) _____
- ✓ Sponsorships and participation in charity/community-oriented events)_____
- ✓ Agency retainer and/or project fee _____

Miscellaneous
- ✓ Other compensations ("shared" sales commissions/bonuses, supervisory salaries, management company fees, legal fees, conventions, meeting attendance)_____
- ✓ Marketing research (agency/consultant fees) _____

✓ Corporate public relations (for developer/owner, tied to project) _____

✓ Collateral additions (package inserts, special items such as resident move-in booklet, and community services such as activity calendar) _____

✓ Promotional giveaways (logo coffee mugs, t-shirts, and so on)

✓ Special projects (contingency for unplanned programming) _
_____

✓ Other special costs _____

Chapter 5:

||||||||||||||||||||||||||||||||||||||||||||||||||||||||||||||||||||||||||||||||||||||||||||||||||||

Researching for Prospects and Competition

It's important to understand the various types of senior housing marketing research available, what it is used for, and when it is useful.

More often than not, after conducting basic "due diligence" research to fulfill a lender's standardized requirements, an attitude of "we'll build it and people will come" seems to prevail for many smaller, senior housing communities.

We also often find someone believing he or she has a great site for a senior living community and, while it meets some of the criteria, many factors for a successful community are missing from the location. The person selling the property has a vested interest in selling and, therefore, may plant the seed that this would be a perfect location for a senior community when there may be many other issues to consider.

Marketing research could seem analogous to fortune telling: someone looks into a crystal ball and predicts the future success of a community. Yet valuable marketing research is far more accurate than tea leaves and fortune telling.

It is important to ask yourself what you need or expect marketing research to accomplish, and also to ask and answer the following:
- How much can you afford to allocate from your budget for marketing research?
- What problems could you encounter or are you encountering that marketing research may resolve or address?
- What is the timeframe?

Unless you happen to have a research background, your best option is to engage a consultant with specific expertise in the senior housing industry. Quality research is not an insignificant expense, but cutting corners could prove disastrous for the future of the community. Good marketing research will pay for itself and then some, but you can also be "research rich" and "cash poor" if you don't understand the types of marketing research needed, and when and how it should be used.

When selecting a marketing research firm and/or candidate, it is important to obtain the following:

- References and proof of expertise in the senior housing field
- Sample of similar work
- Projected budget
- A proposal outlining deliverables and timing

There is a tendency for smaller communities to allocate less to marketing research and rely more on secondary resources available through published reports and services such as Claritas, county and government demographic data, and census reports. While this saves money, the available data is open to interpretation and therefore could be less meaningful and reliable.

Many owner-operators view marketing research as something a marketing staff or administrator can compile. However, there may be biases from those who wish the project to go forward while others may simply skim the surface when what is needed is professional, in-depth research.

How Much Should I Pay?

What is a reasonable fee? Throwing out an arbitrary figure would be useless. Costs differ from region to region and based on the scope of the work.

In addition to the actual research, an established firm may be compensated for travel expenses, long-distance telephone calls, courier and mail expenses, and printing additional report copies. Make sure your contract spells out what is included and what charges are considered "incidental" and billed additionally to the contract price.

Depending on the assignment, good research may take approximately four to six weeks plus time completing a final written report. Fees should include conference calls and/or meetings to discuss findings of the report.

If you believe the findings seem to be based on "generic" market information rather than specifics to your market and your project, it's important to say so. Make sure current field research is conducted rather than pulled from a database of information.

Become familiar with specific types of research, and how and why these research tools are of value. Consultants may vary in their recommendations of the research needed, and it is very important to know what you will need and what you will receive.

Quantitative vs. Qualitative Research

Quantitative research comes down to the "numbers." It is what lenders, investors, and others interested in the bottom line rely upon.

In a start-up community, quantitative research should provide information about the depth of the market to support the potential number of units in your community. People speak in terms of "market saturation" when discussing these issues. Is there pent-up demand as evidenced by waiting lists at existing senior communities? Are there other communities in various planning phases (awaiting approvals or rumored to be in the planning stages)? What is their projected capacity? Among existing communities, what vacancy rate pattern exists? How many units are currently available?

If you are projecting rents for a community, you will want to know what competitors are charging, and what discounts and other incentives are being used to close deals.

Qualitative research is subjective research and offers interpretive data. It assists in planning a community as well as its marketing campaign and may be based on local demographic profiles, sensitivities, and interests.

Is this Community Feasible?

A feasibility study may incorporate both quantitative and qualitative research.

If the analysis is undertaken as a prerequisite to arranging financing, the study should include the following:
- Site evaluation
- Competitive study
- Definition of the market (where will residents come from)

- Local demographics
- Market depth
- Amenities and services that may be appropriate or required
- Pricing
- Minimum resident income requirements

Site Evaluation

The mantra of real estate development, "location, location, location," applies to senior housing as well. Will the proposed site be accepted by the market and compatible with its surroundings? Less desirable neighborhoods are normally not an option for a successful senior community. Residents want pleasant views from their windows. They want to feel safe and secure strolling within the community or near it.

While adjoining residential areas may be desirable for senior communities, there may be a growing demand for urban infill communities where residents can feel part of the ebb and flow of pedestrian traffic. New urbanism-style locations may be perfect for senior housing communities of the future.

Proximity to services desired by seniors, such as medical facilities and drug and grocery stores, will be important as well as availability of public transportation and accessibility to residential neighborhoods. The site must be easily reachable by employees and families, with adequate available parking.

In evaluating a site, it is important to know if local government (including the Planning and Zoning Department) and the surrounding neighborhood are in favor of a senior community. Neighbors may be concerned about increased traffic 24/7 and the noise of emergency vehicles, rather than seeing the value of senior living.

Site evaluation should also include site plan data such as site size, boundaries, site description dimensions, drainage/retention, and current utilization, improvements, surrounding streets, and abutting uses. The site should be reviewed relative to topography and aesthetic qualities, accessibility to major roadways, location relative to other senior communities, proximity to existing and emerging commercial and community facilities, surrounding land uses, and market impact of those uses.

Competitive Study

It is critical to visit competitive communities and this will be part of a market study. A real estate brokerage company representing a seller may include a competitive study prepared by an appraiser. Realize, however, that the appraiser is evaluating the property for comparables—not for competitive advantages and disadvantages.

Seeing competitive communities first hand should include potential interviews with marketing staffs and management to gain insights about the marketplace. Communities often laugh when "suits" stop in, but senior housing personnel often share their information.

Competitive reviews include information about a community's location, size, type and mix of products, pricing, standard features and upgrades, absorption rates, price per square foot, amenities offered, buyer profile, size of units, most popular units, marketing strategies and incentives, and future communities being planned.

A sample competitive review form is included and this should be updated quarterly, regardless if your community is a start-up or well established in the market place.

Figure 5-1. Competitive review form.

Create a spreadsheet to compare your community (subject property) against competitors in the local market. Additionally, it is helpful to create a worksheet for each competitive property and include a picture and/or pictures.

Update competition with field research at least once a year with an in-person visit and supplement with quarterly reviews to learn of price incentives. Date compiled and a contact person is useful as well as keeping ads and brochure copies.

Community Name: _____

Street Address: _____

City: _____

County: _____

State: _____

Zip Code:_____

MSA (municipality):_____

Submarket:_____

Owner:_____

Management Entity: _____

Total # of Apts: _____

Number of Stories: _____

Year Built: _____

Amenities & Services:

    Meals: _____

    Housekeeping: _____

    Security:_____

    Laundry: _____

    Transportation: _____

    Fitness/Exercise: _____

    Activity Areas: _____

    Other: _____

Apartment Mix:

    Apartment Type: _____

    Entrance Fee: _____

    Monthly Rental:_____

    Size: _____

    Monthly Service Fee: _____

    Monthly Fee/Square Feet: _____

Occupancy as a Percent:_____

Summary (what are the strengths/weaknesses of this community when compared to subject community):

_____

_____

_____

_____

_____

Definition of the Market

In marketing speak, "definition of the market" means simply determining where our market will come from, and identifying and quantifying a pool of potential buyers (potential residents). (It is not untypical for someone to think his or her market will come from "everywhere," but this is hardly true. There needs to be some reason for people to seek this particular location.) A more generic definition of a market is: "Potential customers sharing a particular need or want who may be willing and able to engage in exchange to satisfy that need or want." (*Marketing Management*, Philip Kotler)

In the case of assisted living or a continuing care community, target markets may be entirely different—one being frail elderly people living primarily in the immediate area or with families in the subject location versus a more active, senior population in or outside of the subject location.

Craig Smith, president of Integra Realty Resources, Inc. in Sarasota, Florida, suggests that if your market analysis begins with the market and works its way out (rather than beginning with a methodology and imposing itself in), the entire process is revolutionized and it begins where it should—with the consumer.

One often may hear that buyers will come from within a 5-, 10-, or 15-mile radius of the proposed community, but using a radius measurement may provide misleading data. For example, a community in western Broward County would pick up pockets of neighborhoods that would not fit its socio-economic customer profile if it relied solely on radius data. Using county statistics similarly may result in incorrect data which may incorporate census data and projections prepared by government planning agencies.

Creating boundary lines may offer your best estimates of specific areas from which residents can be drawn. Using resources of those very knowledgeable of these target areas is invaluable. You can refine your market area with information from:

- Interviews with local planning officers and realtors
- Senior resources within the area such as Area Councils of Aging
- Hospitals
- Competition

Local Demographics

Once your market area is defined, additional demographic data is needed. You must understand the potential customers in the area where you are building or repositioning an existing community. Typically this information will include age, average income, average number of household members, marital/family status, number of children in the household, education level of the adults, and percentage of people owning versus renting their homes.

Arlene Thompson, of Thompson Consulting, believes that census data can be used in compiling this market analysis for potential development. Number of households, age breakdown, population growth, and ethnic makeup would assist with analysis. Trends become apparent. If an area has retirees to target and there are pockets of either older or younger residents, the age of residents in an area and the number of people in a household would be important. How much people are paying on property taxes is useful information, too, but would require tax record research.

Market Depth

While this sounds like a swimming pool, it actually is an important calculation. What "market depth" implies is whether competitive communities are filing the need within the market place or there is pent-up demand for a new community. Someone asking "How deep is the market?" is asking what percentage of households in a given area will be attracted to the type of housing your community will offer.

We were called by an Illinois builder desiring to build an independent living rental community. He believed he had an ideal location for his community. Cursory research showed that, although he had a good buy on the parcel of real estate, he lacked the necessary surrounding population of elderly and near-elderly people and therefore his market was not "deep enough." The now-famous line from the movie *Field of Dreams*, "Build it and they will come," may not apply to your prospective community. Good marketing research will tell the story.

Amenities and Services

As part of the competitive study and site evaluation, it is also important to focus on what amenities will be included in your community's package. Both to be competitive to other community's offerings as well as to entice potential residents, amenities and services are essential. Many communities provide the obligatory amenities such as multipurpose rooms, craft rooms, dining, and a fitness center. But to be competitive and successful, it is important to know exactly what the competition offers and to what extent, and how well it is received. For example, much like cruise ships that offer "anytime dining," some senior communities may embrace this concept while others have pre-established dining hours and seating. Preliminary planning must determine what the market provides and what the market wants.

Tapping into the external community's amenities and services will prove important as well, and initial marketing research should surface anything in your area that would appeal to your audiences. For example, if your community is unable to include an indoor swimming pool, there may be a nearby athletic complex with a wonderful pool and senior classes. Similarly, state-of-the-art fitness centers, senior centers, and universities may supplement what your community will offer. Opportunities may abound to set your community apart that are in easy reach of your community and can be accessed by your community's transportation.

Pricing and Rates

Lease rates need to correlate to what the market will bear (in other words, what the consumer in your area can afford to pay). Financial analysis incorporates the costs of development, financing, and operations in developing the projections for rental rates. It also takes studying competitive communities to see what fees are currently acceptable to consumers. A well-intentioned developer/owner wishing to "push the envelope" in the market and build a lavish, upscale community may find his building, marketing, and operating costs make his "trophy project" unrealistic for the current market and its location.

Minimum Income Requirements

This refers to what people can afford, not only to live in the community—either in rental costs or the initial costs with on-going maintenance fees of the CCRC—but what financial assets they have in savings, real estate equity, and other forms of income.

Qualitative and External Research

External research is very valuable both in planning a new community and repositioning or improving underperforming sales. Qualitative consumer research, which helps in solidifying customers' interest, is often performed via focus groups, mail surveys, and telephone surveys (which now are expanded with Internet surveys). These common methods all provide helpful insights. Additional research may include mystery shopping, telephone mystery shopping, and audio-video mystery shopping. Area and neighborhood audits are useful, too.

Focus Groups

Both the definition and use of focus groups vary by the consultants employing their use and the communities using them. One differentiation could be "formal" and "informal."

Formal (Traditional) Focus Groups

A traditional focus group may be best used to gauge interest in a new senior community, test participants' reactions, and identify perceived strengths and weaknesses of the proposed community.

A traditional focus group session lasts approximately 90-120 minutes and is lead by a trained facilitator. It involves persons selected for the session based on common demographics, attitudes, or buying patterns germane to the topic. It can either be a full group of eight to ten participants or a mini-group of four to six. Because of typical group dynamics, it is better to have separate groups of men and women. A professional setting is used, including a two-way mirror for observation. Sessions may be videotaped or recorded. Participants generally are paid for their time, and refreshments are provided.

Success depends on the quality and qualifications of the facilitator, who could potentially bias participants if unskilled. The quality of participants is vital, as well. Matching the focus group profile to your prospects and their families is critical. If participants are not similar to your potential customer, they may not provide accurate opinions relevant to your community. For example, if your focus group is researching an upscale, luxury senior community and the entire group is aghast at the price tag, this reaction would only be valid if the participants represent your actual prospects.

Used successfully, focus group research can give a good read on how well your community and product will appeal to the market and other insights into community planning. You can learn, for example, if people prefer pedestal sinks or twin vanities, muted or bright colors, patios and decks, and preferences about menus and recreational activities.

Informal (and Informational) Focus Groups

Informal and informational focus groups similarly are used to gauge interest, but these groups may have more attendees and an underlying intent to build an interest list for the prospective community. In other words, while soliciting opinions you are leveraging the grass-roots efforts of the focus group to generate the first buzz about the potential community and its plans. Informal focus groups are also useful to gauge residents' feelings about a community at various times. By asking key residents to participate in focus groups, you may glean extremely useful information about their take on community issues.

Use of a trained moderator/facilitator is important and we recommend using someone from outside the community. People need to feel they can speak their minds to an unbiased listener. We also encourage a conversational exchange of ideas. These sessions are not videotaped, but discussion notes can be taken or taped and transcribed for future reference.

Surveying by Mail, Telephone, and Internet

Surveys and questionnaires by mail, telephone, and Internet also can be used to gauge interest and provide feedback. E-surveys will possibly become more common as use of the Internet continues to grow among seniors.

Effective surveys depend on asking the right questions and

interpreting the feedback correctly, regardless of the survey vehicle. *Tip:* To achieve a successful survey:

- Know what you need to find out.
- Ask effective questions.
- Determine how the survey will be deployed (community web site, E-mail to past customers, advertisements, and so on).
- Screen respondents to make sure you are surveying the right people.
- Tell respondents how long the survey will take and keep it short.
- Keep the audience interested by asking questions, but not re-asking the same question in a different way.
- Keep the survey easy to use.
- Test the survey before going live.
- Use the data; your findings may be useful for community planning and also great publicity and whitepaper content.

Telephone surveys can be administered via telemarketing, but it is important that participants not feel they are being solicited by fast-talking phone-room callers. Selecting a telemarketing firm requires research on your part. You want to make sure the surveyors assigned to your project are particularly sensitive to speaking with seniors, who are constantly called in telemarketing scams. Today it is important to first obtain permission to call. Thus a telemarketing survey may be used as a successful follow-up tool after some other interaction with the respondent.

Chapter 6:

||||||||||||||||||||||||||||||||||||||||||||||||||||||||||||||||||||||||||||||||||||||||||||||||||||||||||||

Creating a Successful Marketing Strategy and Marketing Plan

A community needs to have a marketing strategy as well as a marketing plan.

To understand their differences as well as how they are related, an analogy may be that of an umbrella. The strategy would be the fabric portion of the umbrella; the marketing plan would be the handle; and all the spokes represent the various actions in the plan to implement the strategy.

Developing the Marketing Strategy

The crux of a marketing strategy is determining how your community will be positioned to attract potential customers and future residents. The marketing strategy defines who you are and better explains what you are really selling.

In a marketing strategy, as you define your community you may also want to think in terms of market dominance. Will your community be perceived as a leader, challenger, follower, or niche? This philosophical question needs to be answered as it will drive marketing efforts.

It helps when considering marketing strategy to think about the essence of what separates one community from others. Many communities market themselves as luxury senior communities. While they in fact may be luxurious, they may find it helpful to go back to the drawing board and brainstorm more of their essence and specifically why one community would be luxurious as compared to another.

Unique Selling Proposition

Part of developing the marketing strategy is creating a unique selling proposition, commonly known as a "USP." Often when asked for the USP of the community, people come up with something related to the sticks, bricks, and mortar rather than translating the unique value of the community.

Value is not only about price. USP relates more to unique character. Perhaps your community offers cutting-edge training for employees to deliver top-notch customer service, continuing education taught by resident professors, pet care including boarding, or flexible dining hours. These are unique features that could be incorporated in the USP.

When potential buyers spread out the informational brochures from several communities on their dining room table and try to narrow their choices, the community with the strongest USP inevitably will win or motivate a return visit.

The USP is reflected in all collateral such as brochures and newsletters, buyer correspondence, advertising, online communication, and in the sales presentation.

Creating a USP can involve a five-step process, according toe Jane Marie O'Conner of 55 Plus Marketing:

1. Know your target market.
2. Explain the benefits your community provides.
3. List the most important and distinctive benefits customers will experience if they move to your community.
4. Define your promise.
5. Combine all the benefits, brainstorm, and narrow to those that are most important.

Target Markets

Determining the target markets draws on the marketing research that has been done to identify potential buyers and develop their buyer profiles.

In senior housing, generally a primary market should come from within the immediate 5- to 10-mile radius. Targeting a primary market is not a scattergun approach. It should focus on specific neighborhoods where people meeting your buyer profile (which would take into account age, income, education, professional background, and religious preferences) may currently reside.

Primary market members share basic common identifiers and similar wants and needs. Secondary target market members may have more diverse characteristics while still offering potential as customers. Reaching a primary market may rely on local advertising, public relations, and promotions while reaching the secondary target audiences would rely more on Internet marketing since they would be dispersed throughout a wider geographic area.

For example, a community planned for a metropolitan city such as New York could first draw on a primary market of seniors currently living in NYC while the secondary market could be people desiring to move back to the city. A senior community in a residential area of a city would typically attract as its primary market people who currently reside in and around the community rather than people from across town. Your city may have dividers that an outsider may not recognize such as the east side of town versus western suburbs. A community with a religious sponsorship could draw from outside its primary market as individuals desire to live with people of the same religious affiliation.

Benefit Selling

Benefit selling is also part of the marketing strategy. The benefits of your community are the real reasons people have chosen your community over others. Why are people coming to work at your community versus another? And why are families selecting it for their relatives.

In brainstorming benefits, it may be helpful to take a feature that your community offers and add the expression "so that" to trigger a discussion of benefits rather than features. For example, a feature of your community might be daily transportation to the town center. You can identify the benefit as "We offer daily transportation to the town center *so that residents can enjoy the independence of easily doing their own shopping and errands.*"

You'll find that most if not all senior communities offer dining, transportation, and housekeeping, but think about how your community dining is different than 10 other communities in the area. If it really is the same, then it may be worthwhile to involve Operations to find some aspect that can be different. Perhaps it is as simple as offering homemade desserts, bread, or ice-cream....or designing the kitchen and dining room to be more homelike so residents can watch daily food preparations.

Branding and Brand Promise

Word about a new community coming to town quickly hits the street—sometimes as early as site acquisition or planning and zoning approvals. Branding of your community begins with its name, so the more quickly a name and identity are selected, the better.

Branding is multi-faceted and involves the company and the community's name and tag line, as well as the "brand promise." Brand promise should have three components: it should be unique, it should be compelling, and it should be believable. Brand promise is about your essence. For example, a brand promise could be that a community is "close to everything." Is this an accurate description? It is believable if the community can be accessed by convenient roadways and is near shopping, recreation, medical facilities, educational opportunities, and residential neighborhoods. But "close to everything" has become a commonplace phrase found in many brochures and ads. It is neither unique nor compelling. A successful brand promise would have all three components.

Your community's name, logo, and tag line help set you apart from competitors. They should reflect the unique character of your community and resonate with the consumers. Hiring a professional to develop these items is of value. They should want to see the site, community plans, and marketing research. They should provide several alternatives to choose from and work with you in finding wording and graphics that fit into the marketing strategy.

Naming and Brand Identity

There are no rules governing whether a community should be known by the corporation's brand name or have a unique community name. National chains such as Classic Residence by Hyatt have strong name recognition and have worked hard in developing their brand. Other communities use an individual name rather than a corporate name. You may also find that regional chains may use the geographic location and tie it to a standard name given to all their communities, such as "[XYZ Community] at [City] location."

Successful names are easy to pronounce and relate to the image of the community, its lifestyle, and theme. Naming a community should not be taken lightly, as the name should endure. A community named "The Willows" would potentially imply that willow trees grow on the site or are characteristic in the town. A tag line tied to "Resort Living" would also imply amenities found in a resort hotel.

Naming a community may take some legwork to the local historical society to find ideas that are reflective of the area, but have been untapped by others.

Developing the Marketing Plan

The marketing plan is the tactics you use to create traffic including timeframe, costs, and sales goals. The marketing plan should be committed to paper. There should be a yearly plan as well as a quarterly and monthly version. Understand that marketing plans vary by community in their scope, tactics, and level of details. But even small communities should have marketing plans. They will give you historical data that otherwise can be long forgotten.

It's helpful to develop a plan as a team effort since staff, such as the Activities Department or Dining, will play a part in implementing elements of the plan. If they are involved from its inception, they will have a better understanding of the timetable involved and can help determine if proposed tactics are even feasible.

Figure 6-1. Sample marketing plan.

COMMUNITY_____

This is the marketing plan for_____

I. MARKET ANALYSIS

    A. Target Market

---

1. We will be renting/selling primarily to (check all that apply):

   Total Percentage

   a. Local area residents   _____
   b. Regional/statewide residents   _____
   c. Other   _____

2. We will be targeting customers by:
   a. Age bracket   _____
   b. Family Status   _____
   c. Children's Ages   _____
   d. Lifestyle   _____
   e. Income level   _____
   f. Interests   _____
   g. Values   _____
   h. Other   _____

B. Competition

1. Who are our principal competitors?

   NAME_____

   ADDRESS_____

   _____

   Years in business_____

   Market share _____

   Pricing/Incentives_____

   Features & Amenities_____

2. How competitive is this market?

   High   _____
   Medium   _____
   Low   _____

3. What are our strengths and weaknesses compared to our competition (consider such areas as location, pricing, reputation, amenities & services, staffing levels per # of residents, etc.)?

Strengths	Weaknesses
1. _____	1. _____
2. _____	2. _____
3. _____	3. _____
4. _____	4. _____

C. Environment

1. The following are some important economic factors that could affect our community's success (such as current and projected senior population in target market, economic trends, real estate market, regulatory climate, etc.)

_____

_____

_____

2. The following are some important legal factors that will affect our market.

_____

_____

_____

3. The following are other environmental factors that may affect our market, but over which we have no control:

_____

_____

_____

II. COMMUNITY ANALYSIS

A. Description

1. Describe your community, including its unique character, features, location, etc.

_____

_____

_____

B. Comparison

1. What advantages does our community have over the competition?

_____

_____

_____

2. What disadvantages does it have?

_____

_____

_____

C. Location/Why should they want this site? _____

Does location fit socioeconomic level? _____

Accessibility _____

Work _____

Churches _____

Travel _____

Shopping _____

Major Roadways_____

III. MARKETING STRATEGIES

A. Image

    1. First what kind of image do we want to have and project (e.g., upscale, all the comforts of home, rich amenities and services, active community, recreation programs, etc.)?

    _____

B. Features

    1. List the features we will emphasize:

        a. _____

        b. _____

        c. _____

C. Pricing

    1. We will be using the following pricing strategy:

        a. Suggested price/monthly rent _____

        b. Annual/other fees _____

        c. Incentives (Describe)

    2. Will our pricing structure be competitive with the competition?

    YES _____ NO _____(Explain)

D. Advertising/Promotion

    1. These are the things we wish to say about the community (our sales message/proposition):

    _____

    _____

    _____

2. We will use the following advertising/promotion vehicles:

    a. Broadcast Media   _____
    b. Direct mail   _____
    c. Special events   _____
    d. Personal contacts   _____
    e. Local papers/magazines   _____
    f. Yellow pages   _____
    g. Special tours   _____
    h. Other   _____

3. These are the reasons why we consider the vehicles we have chosen to be the most effective:

_____

_____

E. Marketing budget (by line item)

F. Financing

Down Payment _____   Cash _____
Apx Monthly Payment _____

G. Sales

Sales Goals   _____   _____
                      (Units)   (dollars)
Weekly/monthly rate to achieve goal: _____

Sales Personnel:
    Compensation
    Bonus

Realtor Sales:
    Commissions

Ongoing Realtor Communications:

_____

_____

_____

H. Marketing Theme:

I. On-Site Merchandising:

Signage_____

Models _____

Landscaping_____

Sales Office _____

Displays _____

J. Collateral
    Brochure
    Other

K. Public Relations

L. Special Events

M. Timetable

Marketing Plan Components

Competition

Collect all the information you can regarding your current competition including those existing and those on the drawing board (pipeline). Including this competitive analysis in the marketing plan is important because competitors may be changing in the marketplace—they may have new incentives and new initiatives that you must counter. Compile this data in a comparative chart format using Excel or a similar program. (If time is of the essence, you may want to consider outsourcing the competitive study.) The comparative chart should include:

- Community name and photo of exterior
- Location with address, telephone number, and E-mail address
- Apartment styles
- Apartment features
- Apartment sizes
- Age of community
- Size of community (acres/number of apartments)
- Price of each apartment style (starting from and range)
- Price per square foot
- Amenities
- Leasing incentives
- Second person fee
- USP
- Source of data

Competitive information is valuable and should be used in sales training to arm sales teams with facts they'll need when a prospect mentions they have visited one of your competitors.

Advertising

Advertising keeps the community in the public's eye. The advertising portion of the marketing plan should show what media placement is planned for the year and what each will cost. It is useful to include the sample ads.

Internet Leads

You may allocate funds to Internet advertising, search engine optimization, and leads generated by online referral companies. This should be indicated on the plan.

Community Outreach

It is worthwhile to allocate funds to charity advertising in the local community, support of a local school, and attending networking events.

Direct Mail

Your marketing plan should include what types of collateral will be mailed and to whom. Include sample letters, post cards, and invitation you plan to use. Even if these aren't completed, include drafts and/or rough layouts

Be sure to include "fulfillment" costs, which are the expenses to sort, affix mailing labels and postage, as well as postage.

Remember, direct mail is not individual mailings that salespeople may do—direct mail is a mail project involving a greater quantity.

Promotions/Events

Events can be large-scale or smaller, simpler gatherings. The marketing plan contains the information as to the event theme but can also include invitations and details on how guests will be invited and related costs. There may be overlap between events and direct mail if invitations are mailed. Take care not to duplicate charges.

Publicity

Plan stories ahead or at least indicate in the marketing plan when there will be a press release. For example, if you are planning an event open to the public you may need to plan pre- and-post publicity. If you want a human interest story placed on behalf of the community, this should be indicated. Ideally there should be at least one public relations tactic each month.

Referral Sources

There should be specific tactics to engage referral sources. These can include external professional sales calls to targeted individuals. This strategy may also incorporate attending various community-based events to network with referral sources. It may be useful to subdivide this tactic with a target list of individuals that are cultivated monthly. Meeting your neighbors may be worthwhile, too, to educate the surrounding neighborhood about your community offerings.

Marketing Budget

As part of the marketing plan, there is a coinciding budget that tracks all expenditures and then there should be a related projection of inquiries and sales. A budget to project results is needed so that expenses are not indiscriminate. Spending $5,000 on an event would hardly seem worthwhile if there was not some thought to the number of people the event would attract and the number of leases which would be attributed to the event.

Chapter 7:

||||||||||||||||||||||||||||||||||||||||||||||||||||||||||||||||||||||||||||||||||||||||||||||||||||||

First Impressions and Setting the Stage

When marketing senior communities, make no mistake—the critical first impressions really do count in influencing someone's decision.

Projecting a favorable image with prospective residents, family members, and other visitors is much like inviting someone to your home. From keeping the front door paint fresh to purging clutter or placing an arrangement of fresh flowers on a table, these extra touches set the stage for success and increase your odds against the competition.

> Once when I accompanied a friend and her parents on a tour of a well-regarded, 10-year-old senior community, I was surprised that, in contrast to my last visit some years ago, the décor and furnishings in the reception area seemed dated and worn. The dramatic silk flower arrangement was no longer there and handmade signs cluttered the front desk. The whispered comments I overheard from the couple reflected their negative impressions. I knew they wouldn't be back.

Sometimes the customer's experience may be slighted in order to make a space workable for staff believing that, when people come for a tour, they can be seated in a community area to sit and talk. This is hardly appropriate. There is much more to the moving decision than taking a tour. Salespeople need all the appropriate tools at their fingertips to best relate the community's story to a customer and effectively conduct discovery.

Welcome Centers

In some communities this area is designated as the "Information Center" or "Sales Office," and some communities may still call this area as such. But by naming this room the "Welcome Center," the philosophy behind its function changes.

The customer's first impression should be to feel welcomed to the community. In pre-leasing and pre-sales, the Welcome Center may be a temporary trailer or an off-site location in an office building or shopping center. Regardless of the location, the Welcome Center should reflect the ambiance of the community. The décor should mirror the community. When the community is completed, displays and furnishings can be repurposed to permanent offices so the expense is not wasted.

Multifamily housing developers/owners have long realized the ongoing need for a Welcome Center because there will always be a need to rent apartments. Senior housing communities are just the same. There will always be leasing and sales to new residents.

Placing emphasis on high-quality furnishings and displays that will endure is worth the expense. Focusing on the long-lasting needs for a location to function as a Welcome Center, where potential customers will first visit, is important from initial planning.

Welcome Center Essentials

What should a Welcome Center contain? While the community's layout and space will dictate how much square footage can be allocated, every Welcome Center needs a few essentials:

- Furniture should be comfortable and versatile. Chairs can be moveable to accommodate additional seating in various offices for families.
- First contact with the customer begins at the reception area desk. A receptionist should be able to see an arriving customer to extend a greeting.
- Sales staff and the sales manager should have offices. Each community will have its own philosophy about using these offices for visitors and may instead designate a central area as the Discovery Center.
- The set-up should offer privacy so that conversations regarding someone's decisions are not overhead by others.

Displays

Why are displays necessary? Customers may not walk up and read the displays, but they serve as reminders to leasing staff; they are their cue cards. Few salespeople will remember to "say it all," but displays help them with key information.

Displays may include the following:
- Floor plans
- Developer/owner story
- Management company story
- Apartment feature listing
- Community features and services
- Community site plan to show building site from aerial perspective
- Clubhouse plan or layout, or building layout
- Location map to show what is in the general vicinity
- Healthcare/wellness story
- Scale model

Figure 7-1. Sample community signage form.

COMMUNITY SIGNAGE

PROJECT: _____

DATE: _____

LEASING INFORMATION	Quantity	Cost
• Snipe directional with arrows		
RIGHT ARROWS	_____	_____
LEFT ARROWS	_____	_____
STRAIGHT ARROWS	_____	_____
• Moveable "A" frame	_____	_____
• Banner	_____	_____
• Hours and telephone	_____	_____
CLUBHOUSE		
• Pool rules	_____	_____
• Mens/Women	_____	_____
(located on bathroom doors)		

- Maintenance Staff Only _____ _____
- Parking for Future Residents _____ _____
- Hours _____ _____
- Resident Criteria _____ _____
- Laundry Room Hours _____ _____
- Meter Room No Storage _____ _____
- Proudly Managed by _____ _____
- No Smoking _____ _____
- ID Required/Company Policy _____ _____

COMMUNITY SIGNAGE
- Fire Extinguishers in Each Unit _____ _____
- Apartment door numbers _____ _____
- Building Signage _____ _____
- Meter Room _____ _____
- Speed Limits _____ _____
- No Parking – please place _____ _____
  Garbage in Container
- Pardon Our Appearance _____ _____
- Leasing Center Directional _____ _____
- Building Directional _____ _____
- No Smoking _____ _____
- Community entry wall signage _____ _____

OTHER

_____

_____

_____

_____

Other Options for Pre-Sales and Pre-Leasing

In pre-sale and pre-leasing periods (also known as "selling blue sky"), it is useful to show what key public areas will look like when they are completed.

Used by hotels, a color board with samples is an excellent tool. An artist's interpretation of public areas is helpful. Even a place setting of the community's flatware, china, and crystal shows the customer attention to every detail.

Virtual reality tours now offer opportunities to "sell the dream" and can be used to walk people through apartment floor plans as well as the clubhouse and streetscape. A flat panel TV or LCD plasma TV is needed and can be utilized for a looping DVD or interactive computer display. The cost is much more affordable than perceived and worth exploring.

Salespeople may find sales tracking maps, showing apartment availability, helpful. In pre-leasing, these are especially important in showing demand by using stick-on red dots for apartments under contract.

If you have limited space, do the essentials. Provide comfortable desks and chairs. Use the brochure for floor plans. Train sales staff to overcome what the community may lack in displays and offices. But a Discovery Area is essential.

In some communities, residents may enjoy the gathering spot of the Welcome Center. They should know they can find coffee and cookies. An open door policy shows friendliness and warmth plus an opportunity to introduce residents to potential newcomers.

While a pre-leasing Welcome Center may not prove as effective for generating actual leases, it offers an opportunity to set the stage for the community and build an interest list. People may wait to see the community become reality before committing to a contract.

For the CCRC/life care community relying on depositors, use of the Welcome Center is essential.

Known as mobile sales offices and modular complexes, these are somewhat costly investments but highly effective. Tour home-building communities for ideas on presentations. Trailers can be finished with a temporary facade, awning, and landscaping. Parking should be provided.

Although they are promoted as turnkey, these mobile sales offices may need further interior design if they are to mirror the community's look. They can be much like a permanent office complete with light fixtures, wallpaper, carpeting, and furnished and equipped offices. Even a model apartment or vignettes of a sample kitchen and bathroom can be created within the trailer set-up.

Off-site Welcome Centers are also very effective and could be a less-costly investment. A nearby shopping center, strip mall, or office center can eliminate the expense of parking lots, trailer improvements, and permits. Ideally, the Welcome Center should have visibility.

One developer lamented when he was told he needed a Welcome Center for pre-sales. However, this is a cost of doing business. A sloppy, ill-conceived center can destroy a potentially successful community. If this stage is poorly executed, the messages that are conveyed to customers could be negative. To get the buzz going, people need to see great "blue sky" images.

Figure 7-2. Welcome Center planning, design, and coordination checklist.

SIGNAGE

	PLANNING	PRODUCTION	INSTALLATION
Street directionals, bootlegs 50% straight/25% left/25% right	_____	_____	_____
Parking	_____	_____	_____
Welcome Center directional	_____	_____	_____
Future Building/ Amenities	_____	_____	_____
Permits	_____	_____	_____

OTHER SIGNAGE

	PLANNING	PRODUCTION	INSTALLATION
Main entry signage	_____	_____	_____
Street signage	_____	_____	_____
Building directory signs exterior	_____	_____	_____
Clubhouse signage	_____	_____	_____
Employee parking	_____	_____	_____
Interior signage package	_____	_____	_____
Flags	_____	_____	_____
Permits	_____	_____	_____

WELCOME CENTER PLANNING

	PLANNING	PRODUCTION	INSTALLATION
Traffic flow program	_____	_____	_____
Directional signage	_____	_____	_____
Parking	_____	_____	_____
Entry sign	_____	_____	_____
with hours			
Reception and	_____	_____	_____
Information			
Reception area	_____	_____	_____
holding areas			
Exterior design	_____	_____	_____
Façade	_____	_____	_____
Landscaping	_____	_____	_____
Parking	_____	_____	_____
Lighting	_____	_____	_____
Walkways	_____	_____	_____
Flags and banners	_____	_____	_____

INTERIOR DESIGN SPACE

	PLANNING	PRODUCTION	INSTALLATION
Window treatments	_____	_____	_____
Entry-reception	_____	_____	_____
Welcome panel	_____	_____	_____
Corporate image	_____	_____	_____
(developer/owner/			
management co.)			
Community	_____	_____	_____
building			
floor plan			
Wellness	_____	_____	_____
Community features	_____	_____	_____
Credibility	_____	_____	_____
Location and area	_____	_____	_____
map features			
Lifestyle photos	_____	_____	_____

Management co. panel – Board of Directors	_____	_____	_____
Floor plan selectors	_____	_____	_____
Standard-option features	_____	_____	_____
Key product-standard samples	_____	_____	_____
Model disclaimers	_____	_____	_____
Amenity story	_____	_____	_____
Renderings	_____	_____	_____
Architectural topographical scale model	_____	_____	_____
Scale models floor plan	_____	_____	_____
Kitchen-refreshment area	_____	_____	_____
Employee lounge	_____	_____	_____
Storage areas	_____	_____	_____
Public restrooms	_____	_____	_____
Copy-mail room	_____	_____	_____
Coat room	_____	_____	_____
Sales offices (closing rooms)	_____	_____	_____
Secretarial area	_____	_____	_____
Conference room	_____	_____	_____
Color selection room	_____	_____	_____

Tips to remember:
- Make sure lighting is sufficient.
- Decorate Welcome Center to blend with color scheme and theme of community décor.
- Display community logo in highly visible and repetitive locations.
- Include logo on wall exhibits.

- Provide casual seating for waiting.
- Have extra seating should family members accompany parents.
- Provide private areas for sales ataff to discuss pricing/health with customers.
- Ensure that offices are well-maintained.
- Service refreshments.

Include:
- Executive desk and chair
- Two guest chairs
- Space for computer, files, and storage

Source: Adapted from the *NAHB Checklist of Shelter Marketing Requirements* and *Sales & Marketing Checklists* by Jan Mitchell

Permanent Welcome Centers

When a community is being planned, it is important to give consideration to how future residents will visit the Welcome Center when it is within the community. Will the receptionist notify the Leasing Department that customers are waiting? Will customers find their way to the Leasing office on their own? Will it be entered from the exterior of a building? Ideally, the goal should be to have salespeople greet customers in the lobby and invite them to the Welcome Center rather than visitors wandering through the building unescorted.

Never lose sight of the value of these first impressions. While it may seem somewhat formal, the community is home to its residents. This is the starting point for someone's future life.

Chapter 8:

|||||||||||||||||||||||||||||||||||||||||||||||||||||||||||||||||||||||||||||||||||||||||||||||||||

Telling Your Story –
From Brochures to All the Trimmings

Despite the growing use of web sites for preliminary research, the senior housing customer may still anticipate receiving some type of printed collateral regarding the community.

An eye-catching ad and web site, with an opportunity to request a brochure with related collateral, are vital in creating first impressions that may precede a visit to the community.

Brochure Collateral

A brochure offers an opportunity to "wow" your audience. It is the "sizzle."

Your customers and their families may obtain a whole host of brochures before stepping foot in the community. These are perused and compared as people ready themselves for the next step—a visit. Following an initial visit, the brochures may be perused further.

A brochure and collateral should reflect your community's image—that is, its unique character. The brochure also positions your community among its competitors.

Initial Decisions

There are some basic marketing questions that need to be discussed when planning collateral.

Content Needs

Do you want the brochure to be a comprehensive information package that provides in-depth information and answers many initial questions? Or do you want it be more basic and stimulate interest to encourage an on-site visit? These decisions involve both the marketing philosophy and cost considerations, and it is important to determine them early.

Distribution

Will the entire brochure kit be mailed to respond to inquiries? Or will a smaller, condensed version be used? There should be a discussion as to price information. Will a price list be mailed for all the floor plans? With the current cost of mailing, will a $5 postage fee be a worthwhile expense for a telephone or E-mail inquiry requesting information? If a tour is encouraged, the brochure kit may also be distributed.

Will inquiries be directed to a web site to download a brochure version?

Brochure Alternatives

A two-prong approach entails producing two types of brochures:
- A less comprehensive or expensive brochure may give a community overview. This is often called a "rack brochure" or "trifold" because it fits in display racks. It can be handed out or used in direct mail campaigns at a relative low unit price.
- A more elaborate brochure package can either be mailed to qualified prospects or distributed to a customer following a tour. It would recap much of what is discussed and provide visual memory of the community.

Brochure Elements

Many of the brochure elements depend on the community's marketing philosophy. During pre-leasing, you may think that it is not necessary to provide a transportation schedule, sample menu, or activity calendar when these have not been finalized. But it is important that people be able to see how their lives will be enhanced by living at the community. Disclaiming these details as "proposed" or "suggested" is a way to safely provide these important brochure elements.

Brochure elements for consideration include:
- General description, philosophy, and community overview
- Floor plans

- Apartment features
- Community amenities and services
- Community site plan indicating residential buildings and integration to the overall community
- Community newsletter
- Sample menu
- Sample activity calendar
- Transportation schedule and routes
- Location map showing conveniences near the community

Figure 8-1. Brochure elements checklist.

This checklist may help in compiling brochure collateral material for a community.

Mandatories
_____Logo
_____Community name _____
_____Community address_____
_____Community telephone _____
_____Community facsimile_____
_____Community web site _____
_____Community Email address_____
_____Fair Housing logo
_____Other logos
_____Directions _____
_____Corporate ownership/management company mandatories

Floorplans
Thoughts may vary on the inclusion of several of these items such as square feet and apartment dimensions. There are differences of opinions on their use by customers.
_____Model names
_____Rendering of building
_____Floorplan locator
_____Apartment features
_____Apartment room measurements

_____Apartment square feet (including or excluding balconies, patios, closets)

_____Show furniture layout

_____Apartment designation (one bedroom/one bath, two bedroom/two bath, etc.)

Other potential brochure inserts

_____Transportation schedule

_____Sample menu

_____Sample activity calendar

_____Sample community newsletter

_____Brochure inserts on medical provisions of community (wellness)

_____Price sheet

_____Community services

_____Community amenities (recreation facilities, recreation center floorplan)

_____Community site plan

_____Community brochure

_____Community tri-fold mailer brochure

_____Area location map

Other

_____Envelope for brochure mailing

_____Kit package to accommodate brochure inserts

Other Items for Consideration

Web Site

An integral part of the collateral is a community web site. While it should mirror the brochure in its look, it offers new opportunities for content that is not completely repetitive of the brochure. Specialists are needed to design effective web sites as there are unique considerations for a site that will attract a growing number of users.

Move-In Booklet

This booklet provides useful information to assist prospective residents planning to move. It would include advice on downsizing and packing, finding a mover, knowing what to expect on moving day, and getting settled. This booklet shows the customer that your staff is caring about them prior to moving. A question-and-answer format is useful along with a checklist. You may want to form alliances with various consultants who specialize in assisting seniors with moving; including their contact information also would be helpful.

Sales-Oriented Newsletters

If budget permits, a newsletter that is created as a marketing tool is extremely useful. This is somewhat different than the community's monthly activity newsletter, which is geared to current residents. Ideally the sales-oriented newsletter could be published on a quarterly basis as an alternative to updating the community's brochure. It may incorporate extensive photography while portraying the lifestyle of the community. Content should radiate the vitality of the community with recent and upcoming events, new services, and inspiring resident stories. The underlying goal is to send a message that "If you lived here, you could be enjoying these great experiences."

Production and Cost Issues

Who Will Write the Copy?

There are times to use specialists and then there are opportunities to save money: collateral copywriting requires professional writers. You or a staff person can draft rough copy and then hire a freelance or agency copywriter to edit this draft. Bring the creative talent to your community. Meet with the writer and tell him or her what makes the community unique or desirable compared with the competition. Provide a tour and pass along any relevant written materials. Review drafts carefully for accuracy and ensure that the writer takes the right approach from the marketing point of view.

> Someone we knew hired a copywriter from the Internet with no knowledge of senior housing or of the specific community. The copywriter was provided brochure samples from competitor communities. The result: while expenses certainly were cut, the brochure copy doesn't whet someone's interest to visit the community. It sounds like every other senior community's brochure and doesn't portray the uniqueness this special community offers.

Who Designs the Brochure or Web Site?

This is the time to hire a freelance graphic designer or design agency. These are specialists familiar with print production. They will usually find a way to work within your budget. Sometimes a freelance graphic designer may be preferable if no additional work, such as ads and media-buying services, is required. Designers have resources with photographers and the extensive photography now available on the Internet. Always look at samples of similar collateral and find work that you like in someone's portfolio before awarding your design project.

It is important to let the designer either control the printing or sign-off on work produced by a printer. To avoid a poor print job, someone needs to take responsibility and be accountable to ensure quality control.

Figure 8-2. Sample brochure.

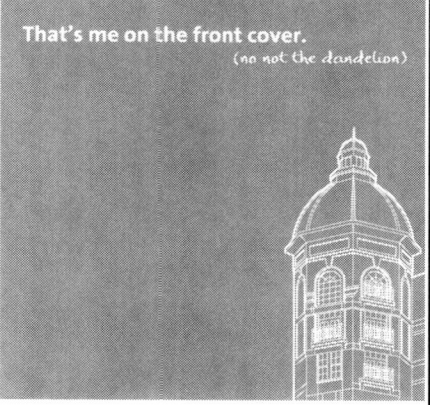

01 let's look forward to looking forward

02 let's be honest (about what we really need)

03 let's live amongst our 'things' without being ruled by them

04 let's be green without envy

05 let's never let a day pass without laughter

06 let's all remember that old age is always 15 years older than I am

07 let's eat like kings

08 let's keep our hearts unwrinkled

09 let's fool gravity

10 let's not have to worry about the 'little stuff'

(1615 Hinman) North Elevation

matherlifeways

The Mather

Introducing the next chapter in the life of those who believe wishes do come true.

Located on the edge of downtown Evanston just two blocks from the lake and Northwestern, The Mather isn't your conventional retirement living experience. It is a forward-thinking solution to the lifestyle desires of today's "emerging" older adults. Not just bricks and mortar, but built upon your fondest wishes. Wishes that spring from your imagination and heart.

Learn the details. Lock in your choice location. Relax, with no cancellation penalties. Receive invites to exclusive events and ongoing updates leading up to the 2009 opening!

Call to receive a priority information package!
Contact us at (847)492.7400

Mapping out your future?

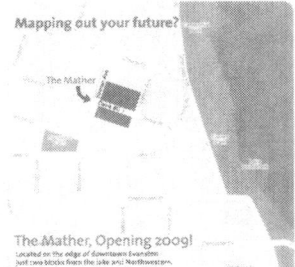

The Mather, Opening 2009!
Located on the edge of downtown Evanston just two blocks from the lake and Northwestern.

We found a place to build your wish on.

What's your wish list?

Call to receive a priority information package!
Contact us at (847)492.7400

Source: Mather LifeWays, Evanston, Illinois

What Is the Appropriate Style?

A brochure should fit the image of the community and it becomes a marketing challenge to create appropriate branding for the community. While a luxury community may need a "wow" package complete with high-quality paper stock, a parchment cover sheet, and watercolor illustrations, a more affordable community may require fewer bells and whistles while still making a nice impression.

Usually the brochure should be four-color and printed on high-quality stock of decent weight and thickness, but creative talent may opt for interesting alternatives in photography and artwork. Because the rack brochure contains similar elements, it should reflect the same look and feel.

Brochure kits with folded flaps that allow you to insert various items (specific floor plans, community maps, special incentives, and so on) are often popular. These inserts can then be updated without reprinting the entire brochure. Include die-cut slits on one of the flaps for business cards. The kit should be a standard dimension to fit standard envelopes if you are planning to mail it.

Think about what the brochure needs to contain when the customer takes it home and how you want it to look. Being able to place various documents in a kit and/or envelope is convenient and creates a nice impression rather than a handful of loose papers.

What Kind of Photography Should We Use?

Use only high-resolution, well-composed photography. Although extensive libraries are now available with user-free stock photography, you must understand the limitations of their use. You may see "your photograph" elsewhere; you don't have exclusive use of these stock pictures.

It is worthwhile to hire a good commercial photographer for on-site work or make sure the design firm coordinates on-site photography. While the initial costs may seem high, over a period of time and multiple uses the resulting photographs become less expensive. Budgets for photography also need to include models, props, and a stylist. Sometimes a creative director may be needed, too.

According to Michael Paras of Paras Photography, NYC, tips for using a professional photographer including determining and negotiating up-front the price, usage, and shoot schedule. When the photographer and modeling agency speak in terms of a "full day," it's important to know the exact start and end times.

Photography and model rights need to be understood, and having this in writing is essential. While you may have paid for the photo shoot, it needs to be clear who has the rights to the photos and can reuse them. Your community may have rights to use the photos for the web site, brochure, newsletter, and local advertising, while a national campaign may not be included in the agreement. It is certainly counter-intuitive, but this is the world of professional photography.

Photographers who are experienced in photographing people are different than architectural or studio photographers and, again, it's important to determine up-front what is needed. It is helpful to have a photographer tour the community before the shoot to plan locations, angles, and the time of day for the shoot.

Many communities feel their residents are the best models and strive to be realistic in portraying the lifestyle. But great care needs to be taken using these inexperienced models. No only is it more time-consuming, feelings can be hurt when the photographer feels a resident really isn't photogenic or wants, for example, to use a wife but not her husband in a particular picture. Be sure to have photo releases signed and ensure that, if a resident is no longer living at the community, the pictures are still useable.

Figure 8-3. Photographic release.

<u>Photographic Release</u>   Date _____

In consideration of my engagement as a model, and for other good and valuable consideration acknowledged as received, upon the terms stated, I hereby grant _____
_____ (the community) and _____
_____ (the agency) permission to copyright and use, re-use and publish, and republish photographic portraits or pictures of me or in which I may be included, in whole or in part, or composite or distorted in character or form, without restriction as to changes or alterations, from time to time, in conjunction with my own or a fictitious name, or reproduction thereof in color or otherwise made through any media for art, advertising, trade, or any other purpose whatsoever.

I also consent to the use of any printed matter in conjunction therewith.

I waive any right to inspect or approve the finished product or products, the advertising copy or printed matter that may be used in connection with or the use to which it may be applied.

I hereby release, discharge and agree to save harmless _____ _____ and all persons acting under the community's permission or authority from any liability by virtue of any blurring, distortion, alteration, optical illusion, or use in composite form, whether intentional or otherwise that may occur or be produced in the taking of said picture or in any subsequent processing thereof, as well as any publication thereof even though it may subject me to ridicule, scandal, reproach, scorn and indignity.

I have read the above authorization, release and agreement, prior to its execution, and that I am fully familiar with the contents.

Resident/Guest: _____

Address: _____

Witness: _____

When a community is in pre-construction, resort hotels in the area may offer an ideal alternative location. Such hotels offer many of the amenities your community will include and are easily approached for a photo shoot.

How Many Should We Print?

If your brochure will have a long shelf life, do not stint on your print quantity. The cost difference between 2,000 and 5,000 copies is relatively low since more of the expense is in creative work, artwork, and photography. Remember to factor in a storage location. When you take into account all the inserts, kits, and envelopes, it's a lot of paper.

Janis Ehlers

How Do We Integrate the Design?

The collateral should work in concert with your letterhead, stationary, and business cards. Ideally your overall planning should allow for consistent color schemes in the community's architectural design and color palette, signage, logo, ads, and promotional materials, including all collateral.

Chapter 9:

||||||||||||||||||||||||||||||||||||||||||||||||||||||||||||||||||||||||||||||||||||||||||||||||||||||

Keeping in Touch – Direct Mail and Its Use

To mail, or not mail—is this your question?

There is really no question that a compelling direct mail letter, targeted to the right list, can increase leads and traffic for your community. So when is direct mail worth the expense? Direct mail is most effective and useful during the lease-up period. When it is tied to specific sales programs, when a community is new, or when a community is underperforming and sales need re-energizing, an effective direct mail campaign is invaluable.

The philosophy of "Once you are on our list, you are here for the duration" is an excellent strategy for senior housing direct mail programs. The person who attends a community event may not be ready at that time to move. A life crisis could change the situation, but that may be years in the future. In the meantime, though, this same person may be an excellent referral resource. Keeping your community's name in front of such people on a periodic basis is like chicken soup for a cold—it cannot hurt and it probably helps. Be assured: one senior tells another.

Today, in addition to print campaigns, direct mail can be done via the Internet. Personalized E-mails, E-blasts, E-flyers, E-invites, and more can supplement a direct mail campaign (although some seniors are careful not to open E-mail from unknown sources). A benefit of Internet direct mail is it goes straight to the consumer.

Tailoring Your Message

Direct mail as a marketing tool has one primary goal: to ultimately create sales. Used effectively, there is a reverberation effect as direct mail creates interest in the community...interest generates traffic... traffic generates sales.

There can be mailings to cold leads that are obtained through the purchase of mailing lists and to warm leads developed from a list of inquiries. To be most effective, a direct mail campaign should be specific to each group and have a message tailored to the audience.

Figure 9-1. Suggested direct mail letter list.

SUGGESTED DIRECT MAIL LETTERS

LETTER	AUDIENCE	PURPOSE
Community concept	Cold Zips	Informational
Thank You/Gen'l	Tel/Mail Query	Accompany brochure
Thank You/Family	Tel/Mail Query	When appropriate
Follow-up (no response)	Tel/Mail Query	Follow-up 1st Thank You
Thank you	Center Visitor	Keep visitor abreast
Community Progress	Past/Cold Zips	Encourage first visit
Professionals	Attys/Drs/Sr Care	Encourage referrals
Thank you	Referral Contact	Appreciation
Project Construction	Cold Zips/Past	Update building opening
New Retiree Living	Cold Zips	Compare rental w/ rental + services
Community Center	Cold Zips	Detail amenities
Published Article 1	Cold Zips/Past	Accompanies project story
Published Article 2	Past/Referrals	Accompanies any senior story
Rabbis/Church Leaders	Personal	Community detail, invites visit
Refresher/Update	Past Traffic	Recapture att'n of early visitors

Alzheimer Letter	Inquiry	Response in some detail to care query
Emphasizes Activity	Cold/Past Traffic	Accompanies first newsletter
Emphasize Way of Life	VIPs/Referral Sources	Accompanies first newsletter
First Bldg Near Opening	Cold Zips/Past	Guarantees pre-public viewing

Cold Lead Mailings

When there are no leads "in the hopper," developing an interest list using direct mail to supplement an advertising campaign is very effective. Philosophically, "you need to start somewhere," and getting in front of potential customers and referral sources is key.

Allocating marketing funds to lead cultivation helps in identifying future target areas and potential audiences. It is sometimes useful to purchase a list geared to a specific target audience, age, and income. Direct mail companies have many criteria to select but as the criteria narrow, the price of the list increases. It may also be worthwhile to purchase a business-to-business mailing list, depending on your location. If you purchase such a list, try to also obtain phone numbers so that the direct mail may be followed up with personal cold calls.

Depending on your knowledge of the demographics of a neighborhood and city, it may not be necessary to income- and/or age-qualify the list. It may be necessary only to mail to single family dwellings and/or multifamily homes within specific zip codes and U.S. Postal Department carrier routes. Local knowledge may show pockets of neighborhoods with potentially older residents who may be ideal candidates.

You may also want to target the area surrounding your location to bring awareness of the community to neighbors. For example, in south Florida a senior community located on a site across from the ocean could target many of the surrounding apartment condominiums in a direct mail campaign, knowing that the majority of these residents are older retirees.

It is worth comparing the fees of several direct mail companies and also finding what services they include. Many also offer printing services and thus are a one-stop proposition. However, it is important to verify quality and not sacrifice quality for price.

It is important to track response from these early mailings. Response predicts future success or disappointment. While it may require at least three mailings to spread the word, each mailing should create an increase in inquiries as mail is received. If you have mailed to a list with little qualified response, do not use this zip code in the future.

Warm Lead Mailings

These direct mail efforts target prospects who have expressed interest and/or come through your door. The fresher the lead, the more frequent you should mail to this group. These are folks who have expressed strong interest in the community and are potentially qualified. Direct mail may include thank-you notes, community updates, newsletters, invitations to special events, reprints of relevant articles, and selected press releases.

It is useful to periodically purge the mailing list with interest surveys and inquiry letters to make sure recipients are still interested.

Direct Mail Costs

Although typically very cost-effective, there are expenses associated with direct mail. (A helpful reference is *The Small Business Guide to Advertising with Direct Mail* available through the U.S Postal Service.) Consider the following when using direct mail:

- Creative concept
- Design and production
- Mailing costs
- Mailing lists (purchase/rental/existing)
- Processing labels
- Letter shop production (insertion, sorting, affixing postage)
- Postage

If direct mail projects are planned, develop them in progressive stages for greater reinforcement and continuity of your message and branding.

Another issue to take into account when planning your mailings is when to use first-class postage versus third-class or bulk mail. One yardstick to use is time value: if you are sending an invitation to an event, you want to guarantee it is received well in advance of the event. First class offers this advantage.

Bulk mail may be perceived as "junk mail" and this could negate the effectiveness of the direct mail effort. The odds that your non-first-class mailings are read can be improved to some extent by the quality of the envelope (paper stock and design) and the copy of the "teaser message" printed on the face of the envelope.

What to Mail

Keep in mind the "rule of seven." Studies indicate that you have about seven seconds to engage someone's attention and our short-term memory best handles about seven pieces of information. If you are sending a letter, make it brief and compelling. A paragraph about what makes your community distinctive and why someone would feel right at home would be perfect copy.

Remember—seniors are just like the rest of us. They do not like being inundated with junk mail. If you are going to use direct mail, use it well and wisely.

Send brochures to respond to requests for information. These packets need to be geared to the specific request since, ultimately, a visit to the community is most desirable and more and more seniors are seeking brochure information online.

Some other tips from the U.S. Postal Service and from experience include:

- Don't say too much. Two or three pages, front and back, are overkill and a waste of money.
- Avoid hard-to-read and small typefaces such as script and type size less than 12 points.
- Less is more. You want to interest readers and motivate them to call and visit.
- Even though you are sending a form letter, make it seem as if you are engaging the recipient in a personal letter. Take

advantage of letter template suggestions and adapt them to a specific reader.

- Avoid dense and monolithic blocks of type. Leave ample white space and use bullets to make your main points jump from the page.
- Use words that excite and interest; paint a picture with adjectives.

Figure 9-2. Sample direct mail.

Source: By Design Solutions, Princeton, New Jersey

Postcards

A growing approach in direct mail is the use of postcards. These are a personal favorite due to low mailing costs and high effectiveness. Postcards are fast and cheap, and they get read. If used as invitations, they seem to easily find their way under a refrigerator magnet as a reminder to attend. Postcards are rarely trashed without a curious glance.

Figure 9-3. Sample postcard invitation.

This holiday,
give yourself the
gift of a lifetime.

Visit us at our Holiday Open House and enjoy refreshments, tour the community, and discover how you can retire in luxury while maintaining control of your healthcare choices and your finances. Ask about our year-end specials, and learn how the retirement of your dreams has never been more affordable.

PRINCETON WINDROWS
2000 Windrow Dr., Princeton, NJ 08540
www.princetonwindrows.com

Source: By Design Solutions, Princeton, New Jersey

Effective postcard tips include:
- Keep the message brief with a strong call to action directed to calling or using the web site landing page.
- Use one dominant feature, such as a headline or picture, and don't compete with it.
- One strong photograph is better than a collage of pictures.
- Effectively use both sides of the postcard.
- Have the call to action clear and easy to read.
- If the postcard contains an offer, it should be time-sensitive rather than open-ended.

Chapter 10:

||||||||||||||||||||||||||||||||||||||||||||||||||||||||||||||||||||||||||||||||||||||||||||||||||||||||

Advertising Strategies for Your Community

While adverting dollars in newspapers and magazines have been decreasing with the growing acceptance of the Internet, for the senior housing customer reading the morning newspaper has not gone by the wayside.

Print advertising still effectively reaches the senior consumer and potential referral sources. Does it produce inquiries and traffic? That's where many variables come into play as to advertising frequency, placement, and effective, creative message and design.

Differences between Advertising and Publicity

There is a common misconception differentiating advertising and publicity. Advertising is fee based. Space in a newspaper or publication is purchased generally through a contract. There is a guarantee the ad will appear on the scheduled date. Cost is based on the ad size and day the ad may appear as well as frequency of the ad placement. Frequency is integral to a successful advertising campaign.

Publicity offers no guarantee that an article about your community will appear when desired or how it will actually read. Publicity is gained either through a press release or query to a reporter to write his or her own story. It is a third-party endorsement. Publicity offers a 70% greater retention rate than an ad and basically is free press. When someone says "I read about the community in a positive light," the memory of this article is far more lasting than someone who says they saw your ad.

Janis Ehlers

Media Budgets and Media Buying

After staff salaries, generally one of the largest marketing expenditures is print advertising. While this cannot be deleted from a marketing plan, making advertising dollars go farther is essential.

Begin developing a media plan that shows how much various media will cost for different size ads and placement. A first attempt at a media plan may be too expensive, but needs to be compiled to determine what can be cut.

Figure 10-1. Sample media schedule.

MEDIA SCHEDULE
January – June

Print Advertising:	Circulation or Audience Reach	Size of Ad or Length of Spot	Special Section (if applicable)	Cost	JAN	FEB	JUN	TOTALS
Name of Publication								
Name of Publication								
Name of Publication								
Online Advertising:								
Name of .com								
Name of .com								
Name of .com								
Name of .com								
Radio Advertising:								
Name of Radio Station								
Name of Radio Station								
Television Advertising :								
Name of Television Station								
Name of Television Station								
Outdoor & Transit Advertising:								
Board Location								
Board Location								
Shopping Mall Kiosks:								
TOTALS:				$0	$0	$0	$0	$0

Source: Carlson Communications, Richard G. Carlson, President

Ultimately, advertising will be building name awareness. Print advertising should produce traffic and telephone calls, but ads may appear for weeks without creating a stampede to your door. Building an image takes time.

Many advertising people ask clients what is their media budget, but if you are novice you may not have a clue how much is needed to be allocated to the media budget.

Professional media buyers may not fully understand what needs to be accomplished in the media plan for your community. You must educate them since senior housing is a unique commodity.

Agencies may earn a commission on advertising that is placed, so it is important to carefully critique their recommendations. The agency may encourage you to "go to the max" with four-color, full-page ads without shopping for more cost-effective advertising alternatives.

A talented media buyer needs to understand the timeframe of the community's leasing efforts and develop a plan that is comfortable for everyone.

If you decide to tackle your own media buying, first get to know your advertising representatives at the local newspaper and community publications. Be sure they understand your goals, listen to their recommendations, and tap into their knowledge. Be sure to tour them through the community and educate them on senior housing since most may not be familiar with the concept. But understand they may not have your pocketbook in mind when making recommendations. They also make money on the advertising they sell.

An advertising rep can be a friend and a valuable source of information; they may know about your competition and upcoming expenditures. In addition, your advertising rep may offer the services of the publication's creative department to produce your ad or help you create one. While this offer may sound enticing, understand that the creative person on staff is handling any number of ads for products and services. It is unlikely he or she can offer an ad which conveys the special essence of your community with a compelling message. Spending money for a professional designer is well worth the expense.

Selecting a Creative Team

When you are scouting out agencies, look for a good fit. How many senior accounts they are handling is not as important as how sensitive they will be to your audiences and budget, and their ability to be creative and meet deadlines.

Reviewing a portfolio is essential because you want to see if you like their overall creative look for their clients.

Experience has shown that few creative shops do "spec campaigns" to win business, but it may depend on the potential budget. You may want to consider several agencies and offer a presentation fee to each. If they know you are willing to pay, they may be more inclined to show you a sample ad.

When interviewing, feel out the creative team's understanding of seniors. Can they relate to your senior audience? Do you get a sense that senior communities would be low on their lists of "cool projects"? Ask if their grandparents are alive and what can they tell you about their grandparents' lifestyle or their own parents.

Meet the entire team who will be working on your account—not just the company president. Tour their offices to see if the environment feels creative and friendly. When you look at their portfolio, keep an open mind. Consider what worked for a given product and audience, and not just whether you think a particular ad would work for your audience. See how creative challenges were handled. And while awards are nice, they do not necessarily translate to sales success. Results are of paramount importance. Ask about the results for a particular ad.

If your community is established, have the creative team come for a meal and tour the community; let them sit in on an activity. Create an informal focus group with the copywriter and several residents. Not only will your residents be more forthcoming in providing feedback, the insights into their way of thinking will greatly impact creative thinking.

> A copywriter who was new to working on a senior housing account toured a CCRC and met several residents. At that time he was well into his 60's, but he commented, "I never want my life to be like that." We knew we needed to find another copywriter who would instead say, "I wish I could live that way."

Creative people tend to forget about their own real-life grandparents and relatives and, as soon as they need to think about a senior housing community, their stereotypical image is a television character from *Little House on the Prairie* rather than *The Golden Girls*.

Senior communities are for real people: someone's grandparent and someone's mother and father. A creative person needs to think in terms of people in malls, restaurants, grocery stores, gyms, and on tennis courts. Advertising directed to seniors needs to reflect that reality and understand the hot buttons of the consumer.

When interviewing agencies and creative boutiques, be sure to talk about price and even take a look at a client's bill.

Additional Tips

Pitfalls to avoid include:

- Ads with too much copy (also known as "kitchen sink" ads)
- Too little white space and too much clutter
- Trite photography
- Unclear messages
- Talking down to customers
- Telephone numbers that are hard to find and read

When viewing a proposed ad, be sure to see it in the size that will actually be used. A full-page concept could adapt entirely differently as a much smaller version.

Be prepared to use an ad over a substantial period of time. Why? Your leasing staff may tell you the ad needs to be changed, but often it takes numerous exposures of the ad to produce results. On the other hand, if the ad appears to have run its course and is not generating fresh leads, it is time for a change.

When working with the creative time, your homework should include providing background information. The community's fact sheet is essential as are information about the target market and competition, the project benefits, and your unique selling proposition (or USP, which is how your community is differentiated from the competition). There should be clear understanding of the ad's call to action—what you want the reader to do after reading the ad.

Chapter 11:

||||||||||||||||||||||||||||||||||||||||||||||||||||||||||||||||||||||||||||||||||||||||||||||||||||||||||||||||||

Internet and Social Media –
Evolving Marketing Opportunities

The expression "We've come a long way" certainly holds true for Internet advertising and in a few years may for social media, also.

The first edition of *Marketing Seniors Housing* touched on web sites and when the book was published in 2002, it was fairly progressive to have a web presence. Today it is a prerequisite. In 2002 our focus groups would rarely surface Internet surfers. Today it is unusual to *not* find seniors and their children using the Internet to assist with their senior housing research and decisions.

There are articles, books, webinars, and specialists devoted to specific topics related to E-commerce, the Internet, and social media, and it is important to continue to be aware of and embrace this new world of opportunities. Just as it is vital to incorporate offline tactics into the marketing plan, you must also begin to focus more and more on online marketing and make it part of the strategic marketing for your community.

Many opportunities require baby steps. Rather than simply think that this new world is only for the young or will not influence senior housing customers, it is better to embrace it and keep exploring opportunities.

Web Sites

To recognize its value, realize that a web site captures your prospect's attention when they *want* information. No other type of advertising relates to customers on *their* terms. Remembering this distinction will help in the overall messaging of a web site along with justifying the investment expense.

A web site may be the first introduction someone will have to your community before receiving a brochure. Therefore, the care you take in its design is important. An effective site needs to be continually evolving and updated to retain freshness. Two to three years is the approximate life of a good site and frequent updates during that time are important.

Figure 11-1. Sample web site questionnaire.

WEB SITE QUESTIONNAIRE

Community's URL(s), intended or existing:

What is the desired launch date for the new web site?

Who will be the primary contact for this project?
Name: Company:
Email: Phone Number:

Who will be the technical contact within your company?
Name:
E-Mail: Phone Number:

Strategy
Audience
- Who are your target audiences and what are their characteristics?

Web Usage Skills:	**Age:**	**Gender:**
☐ Novice	☐ 30-40	☐ female
☐ Intermediate	☐ 40-50	☐ male
☐ Pro	☐ 50 +	

Location(s):

Occupation(s):

Income Level:

Other:

- Check all adjectives that describe how you want your web site to be perceived by your audiences.

  ☐ friendly   ☐ progressive   ☐ serious   ☐ humorous

  ☐ casual   ☐ colorful   ☐ technical   ☐ informative

  ☐ professional ☐ smart   ☐ elegant   ☐ playful

  ☐ other:

- How is your community currently perceived?

- What is the key reason your home buyers choose to live at your community?

  ☐ price   ☐ service   ☐ location   ☐ value   ☐ amenities

  ☐ other:

Reasons for developing a web site for your community:

- What are the main reasons for developing a web site for _____?

☐ Reach Different Audience

☐ Expand Business

☐ Expand Services

☐ Competition has Web Site

☐ Add to Professionalism

☐ Other:

Goals

- What goals would you like to achieve with your new web site?

Primary:

Secondary:

- What is the primary "action" the user should take when coming to your web site? (download floor plans, fill out contact form, search for information, etc.)

Competition

- URLs of your Online Competitors (Can be non-competitor web sites). What do you like or dislike about these web sites and why?

URL:
I like their:
☐ color palette ☐ usability ☐ layout ☐ content ☐ navigation
☐ other:

I dislike their:
☐ color palette ☐ usability ☐ layout ☐ content ☐ navigation
☐ other:

URL:
I like their:
☐ color palette ☐ usability ☐ layout ☐ content ☐ navigation
☐ other:

I dislike their:
☐ color palette ☐ usability ☐ layout ☐ content ☐ navigation
☐ other:

- How will community differentiate itself from its competitors offering similar homes and lifestyle?

Web Site Content
Preferences
- Which visual elements, if any, would you like to use from the current web site?
  ☐ logo   ☐ fonts   ☐ color scheme   ☐ photos
  ☐ other:

- Color Preference. Please check all that apply.
  ☐ Required Colors – Pantone #:
  ☐ I'm open for suggestions.   ☐ Web Designer's Decision.
  ☐ Warm Colors   ☐ Cool Colors (blue, green)
    (red, brown, orange)
  ☐ Classic Colors   ☐ Modern Colors
    (black, white, grey)

☐ Oriental Colors
  (red, black, orange, white)
☐ National Colors
  (red, white, blue)
☐ Other:

☐ Playful/Primary Colors

☐ Neon Colors

Design Content
- Web Site Content/Copy.
☐ Have all content/copy approved and ready for delivery.
☐ Have majority of content/copy approved.
☐ Only have small portion of content/copy.
☐ All web site content/copy needs to be created new.
☐ Content will be created in-house.
☐ Content will be created with the help of an outside provider.

Site Architecture
- Do you already have a sitemap or outline for the proposed web site design?
  ☐ yes   ☐ no

- What will be the main categories or sections on your web site?

- What content would you like to see on your web site? Check all that apply.
  ☐ About Us
  ☐ Directions
  ☐ News & Events
  ☐ Newsletter
  ☐ Contact Us
  ☐ On-site Amenities
  ☐ Testimonials
  ☐ Community Work

  ☐ Services
  ☐ Site Plans
  ☐ Pricing & Availability
  ☐ Property Features
  ☐ Floor Plans
  ☐ Development Team
  ☐ Special Promotion
  ☐ Awards
  ☐ Other:

Interactive

Check all that apply. I would also like to have:

☐ Blog ☐ RSS Feeds
☐ Calendar of Events ☐ Contact Form
☐ Video ☐ Photo Gallery
☐ Other: ☐ 3-D Virtual Tour

- Will you have database functionality?
☐ Yes. Please check all that apply. ☐ No
☐ Member Login
☐ Dynamic Content Generation
☐ Search Capability
☐ Other:

- Would you like to have Flash Animation on your web site? Check all that apply.
☐ All Flash Web Site ☐ None
☐ Some Flash ☐ Please advise
☐ Flash Portfolio ☐ Flash Navigation

Evaluation

Please list 10-25 keywords or keyword phrases that relate to your community:

- Is all your content, both text and graphics, in electronic form? Will you need to have photos or artwork scanned into electronic format?
☐ Yes, all is in electronic format.
☐ No, will need some scanning.
☐ No, all will need to be scanned.

- Do you need assistance from a photographer, for example to capture your staff, communities, or properties?
☐ Yes ☐ No ☐ Please advise.
☐ Prefer to work with stock photography (additional charges may apply).

☐ Have Images/Photography and will provide via FTP/E-Mail/ Mail/Drop-off.

Maintenance
- How often will your web site be updated?
  ☐ Weekly ☐ Bi-Weekly ☐ Monthly ☐ Quarterly
  ☐ Bi-Monthly ☐ Yearly ☐ Daily ☐ Other:

- Who do you foresee maintaining your web site?
  ☐ Will maintain in-house
  ☐ Will be outsourced
  ☐ Please Advise
  ☐ Other:

Web Site Marketing
- What methods of distributing your web sites URL already exist on and offline?
  ☐ eNewsletter ☐ Stationary and Business Cards Promotion
  ☐ Direct Mail ☐ Register with Search Engines
  ☐ Place Ads ☐ Other:
  ☐ Web Banner

Additional Comments/Notes:

Source: Carlson Communications, Richard G. Carlson, President

While it was formerly sufficient to have your web site simply reflect your brochure content, a web site is not a brochure and should not rehash brochure information and feature lists. Sites now need these characteristics to be effective:
- Well designed
- Easy to navigate
- Engaging to users
- Updated with news and information
- Call to action

Web sites require designers, but web designers may not know your business or your customer. It's important to educate them about your potential customer and how they would be using a site. People will glance at a page, scan for information they want, and click to discover greater details. Images are more eye-catching than paragraphs of copy. Conveying your community in pictures can be much more effective. Reviewing competitor sites is important as well as sites of leaders in the industry.

If you have only one community, it is much easier to create an effective site. Multiple communities in various geographic areas of the country become more challenging since there is a corporate brand identity as well as individual communities which need to offer information. When developing your web site strategy, remember the end user of the site and how they will be attracted to it. If the community has a well-regarded name while the corporate entity has less identity, this also needs to be taken into account.

Tips to reenergize a web site:
- Continually update with articles and reprints.
- Create a community blog with regular postings.
- Add video footage to show community lifestyle.
- Use testimonials from residents and families.
- Post YouTube clips.
- Post event photos.
- Post current calendars of activities.
- Offer incentives for gifts such as a brochure on moving tips.

Finding a Site

Just like other forms of advertising, prospects need to be directed to a web site. This can be done either offline by reading something and then visiting the web site or online through a search engine. Here are a few tips:
- Include the web address on all community materials including business cards.
- Take advantage of free listing sites as well as referral web sites.
- Use online public relations.
- Think in terms of search engine optimization (SEO) and either

paid search advertising or organic results which occur naturally because your web site is updated with new information.
- Take advantage of social media (such as Twitter, LinkedIn, Facebook, and YouTube).

E-Leads

It is important to not only drive traffic to the web site, but also to get your arms around the E-lead process. The E-lead registration form should be easy to fill in and not require extraneous information. It is important to monitor E-leads as a source of traffic and know how many are being received each month.

There also should be an E-lead follow-up program. These are generally "hot" leads and care needs to be taken that they do not fall through the cracks but instead are quickly supplied the information requested. An automated response mechanism is worthwhile since E-leads may come in during off hours and holidays.

E-Mail Marketing

If your customers are communicating with you electronically and their addresses are captured, it can be effective to keep in touch with them via E-mail. Periodically monitoring E-correspondence between salespeople and customers is worthwhile. Sometimes the tone and content of staff messages may need some tweaking. People need to be reminded to use spell check and to reread their outgoing E-correspondence before clicking Send.

It may be helpful to generate standard templates that can be used in E-correspondence so that salespeople can quickly send thank you notes and community updates.

E-Mail Blasts

From postcards to invitations and newsletters, the Internet can be used to disseminate information to customers. There are special distribution web companies that can be used if a database becomes too unwieldy. You can also simply send E-mail to key names from your address book. Be sure if you are using an address book to blind copy everyone rather than show everyone's name.

Here again, keep it short and creative. Over time you will reap rewards. This is an excellent tool to communicate not only with customers but referral resources, as well.

Blogging for Communities

While updating a web site may require professional services, posting to a blog is an excellent way to inform, educate, generate conversation, and create new pathways to communicate. A blog or even several blogs can be used by a community for a variety of topics. Blogs offer an opportunity for a more casual, informal writing style and, to be effective, should be more informative rather than sales-oriented. It is helpful to review other community web sites and their blogs to get an idea of what you find appealing.

A blog strategy should be part of the marketing plan. Some key tips:

- Plan to post commentary at least twice a week.
- Plan subject matter in advance.
- Select topics that are relevant, interesting, entertaining, and current.
- Designate appropriate people to write for the blog.
- Add photos to make the blog more interesting.
- Keep it short—you can always post again.
- Promote the blog.
- Link to articles and web sites offering readers resources.

Tip: The Flip Video™ camcorder is very helpful in taping short video clips and allows a user to upload directly into the computer to incorporate interviews, events, testimonials, and more into a blog.

Getting Social

Before launching social media initiatives, it is important to create a social media policy for employees as part of your employment policy. There are samples online. Employees should understand that their posts should bring value to the blog.

Residents, family members, and visitors, as well, need to be informed if their pictures are posted online. Privacy should always come first as well as upholding the dignity of residents.

Figure 11-2. Sample Social Media Policy.

Introduction

Social media such as Facebook, MySpace, Twitter, YouTube, and blogging are powerful communication tools that allow you to reach a larger audience than has ever been possible before. The Company respects your right to utilize social media but you must bear in mind that the content you produce may have a profound effect on the Company, its relationships with customers and clients, and its overall well-being. With that in mind, any employee who fails to adhere to any of the Company's expectations with regard to online social media behavior will be subject to discipline up to and including termination.

Our Expectations for Employees' Personal Behavior in Online Social Media

1. **Ethical Behavior.** Always adhere to the Company's Code of Business Conduct, its Anti-Harassment policy and its Anti-Discrimination policy. The Company has zero tolerance for behavior that is harassing, discriminatory, offensive, illegal, or disparaging of any person or company and that applies in cyberspace the same as it applies in the workplace.
2. **Personal Responsibility.** Remember that YOU are responsible for your actions. If you post anything that may tarnish the Company's image, you will be responsible for that act the same as if you had said it directly to your supervisor or other employer. We encourage you to participate in online social media spaces but we urge you to do so while exercising sound judgment and common sense.
3. **Transparency.** If you decide to endorse or provide a testimonial with regard to the Company, its products, any of our competitors, or their products you must identify yourself by name and as an agent of our Company.

> 4. **Protection of Privacy.** Do not at any time disclose information that is confidential, including proprietary company information, customer information, supplier and vendor information, personal employee information, pricing information, information that is copyrighted or trademarked, and any other information not generally available to the public.
>
> <u>Acknowledgement</u>
>
> I have read, understand and agree to follow the Company's Social Media Policy as a condition of my continued employment.
>
>
> _____   _____
> Signature   Date
>
> Source: Alaniz and Schraeder, LLP

Social Media Sites and Their Use

Want to engage grandchildren? Help a grandmother use Facebook or Twitter. Want to spread the word for employment opportunities? Try LinkedIn. Have a great video clip from a recent TV show? Put it on YouTube. Want to start a blog? Try Wordpress or Blogger. Want to improve pictures and share them online? Try Flickr or Picasa.

It may seem daunting, but social media also requires a strategy. Social media offers an opportunity for meaningful engagement with people who can influence the customer as well as interaction with customers themselves.

Social media offers a wealth of opportunity to develop friends, followers, and fans, but it is a 24-7 proposition.

The most important keys to social media success are to keep it real. Social media really is an online version of word-of-mouth marketing.

Some communities are designating a social media staff member to manage these communication vehicles on a daily basis. This task can also be outsourced as it can seem very overwhelming as well as time consuming. Burdening an activity director with social media responsibilities may not be the right fit. The person who is a high-energy, creative type who enthusiastically engages residents may not be adept with Facebook and Twitter.

Remember that social media takes time to produce results. It may be difficult or impossible to quantify and justify it in terms of number of leases that will be signed. Many in management will be tempted to veto its use, but long-range and effective social media use will continue to grow. Thus it is important to embrace social media and Web 2.0.

Chapter 12:

||||||||||||||||||||||||||||||||||||||||||||||||||||||||||||||||||||||||||||||||||||||||||||||||||||||||||||||||||||||||||

Public Relations – The Most Valuable Tool

When it comes to successfully launching a new senior community, repositioning an under-performing or older community, or simply continuing to bring new traffic to the door, never underestimate the value of effective public relations, or PR.

How does PR work in promoting a senior housing community?

Some may explain it in terms of getting your community's name in the news in a positive way. PR is also known as press relations or media relations, but media relations is only one aspect of public relations. PR can be a much more all-encompassing marketing tactic. It helps in giving a community its leg up against the competition and helps the community stand out. It should make the community more interesting to buyers.

Today effective PR employs the Internet as well as traditional print and electronic media. It may encompass community relations and customer service. Public relations is also used for crisis communications, as well.

Who Is Responsible for PR?

An essential decision is whether the community will undertake public relations efforts and, if so, who will be responsible. Will a PR consultant be used or in-house staff, or both? If it is determined this will be a function handled in-house, does the person have extensive experience or will a consultant assist in training him or her?

Starting Off with Good PR

For a new community, effective PR efforts will create brand awareness and relationships that will determine the community's success for years to come.

Define the Publics

It is important to first define the *publics* (aka, the audiences) and then strategize PR plans to reach each one effectively.

Potential publics can include:
- Prospective residents
- Current residents
- Residents on contract (depositors)
- Prospective residents' families
- Neighbors of the community
- Local businesses
- Community activists and movers-and-shakers
- Trade associations and business groups
- Local government (elected officials, department heads, and agencies)
- Area medical community, including hospitals
- Churches and religious leaders
- Employees
- Prospective employees

Think about the best vehicles for reaching each of these audiences. What is used for one group may overlap with others. Newspaper articles can be a great way to generate favorable PR. Key time periods and milestones lend themselves to press release coverage.

Designate a Spokesperson

There should be an individual selected who will be the spokesperson for the community in good times and bad. This is the person quoted in press releases and is the go-to person who speaks on behalf of the community. This person would talk with a reporter needing specific information and, in times of a crisis, would also be the face of the community.

Establish and Communicate Media Policies

It is important to address the community's media policy during employee training. All employees should know who the spokesperson is for the community and also know they are not at liberty to speak on behalf of the community themselves. Employees need to understand how to handle press inquiries as well as an unannounced TV camera crew showing up.

While it is important to respect the privacy of all residents, be careful that you do not miss or mishandle opportunities to achieve positive PR on behalf of the community.

Reporters should not be allowed to wander halls unescorted, and business cards and names should always be obtained.

Figure 12-1. Sample media relations policy.

MEDIA RELATIONS POLICY

To maintain a successful relationship with media, all employees need to understand and follow this policy:

1. Under no circumstances should any employee attempt to answer any question or act as spokesperson for _____ or one of their communities. **All media requests for information must be referred to the corporate office of _____.**

2. If a media representative (reporter, photographer, etc.) seeks entry to a community, they must identify themselves and provide evidence of corporate permission for such a visit. All media people must be escorted by an appropriate community representative at all time while on community grounds. No self-guided tours or simple "walking the grounds" is permitted without escort.

3. Take the name and business card of each person for those who say "We're here with the press." Many people with no legitimate media ties use this phrase to gain access to the community, especially when a special event is being held.

4. Any resident or community employee must be asked permission by the media to be photographed and/or quoted. If you are asked to sign a release form and do not understand why, check with a community official to determine what you should do.

---

5. The offices of _____ (person) will monitor all situations, which involve media on community property. For example:

   a. A press release sent on behalf of the community may initiate a press inquiry directly to you. If so, it is acceptable for you to say, "I'll get back to you," rather than feel pressured to give an immediate answer.

   b. In an emergency or temporary crisis, it may be necessary to issue a prepared statement on behalf of the company. **This is the only permitted response to the media in these situations.**

6. Approval to speak to the media must first be granted through the offices of _____ (person). It is helpful to provide details of what the story is about and the type of questions the reporter will ask. If you do not wish to screen the request in this way, please refer the caller to _____. **Do not speak to the press "off the record"; statements such as these are often later used against the interests of the company and/ or employees, the community and its residents.**

7. In crisis situations:

   A "crisis situation" is defined as any incident, which can place an employee, or resident in a threatened position: a hurricane, fire, or natural disaster. Vandalism, theft, killing, or any kind of controversial event attracting media coverage. In these cases, it is vital to follow these guidelines:

   a. Immediately establish a single company spokesperson, i.e., normally _____ (person). He/She will also determine if a corporate spokesperson is necessary.

   b. If _____ (person) is unavailable, check with a superior for guidance in this regard.

   c. At the time no official spokesperson exists, answer all press inquiries: "As soon as an appropriate spokesperson is available, we will notify you." This is often a preferable answer to protect the employees and/or residents, especially in time of an emergency. Take the name and number of the caller and provide this information to the office of _____ (person) or the appropriate spokesperson.

> d. For a crisis situation, an on-site manager may determine where to establish a media center where the press can be located. This area can be located on the street or in private property, away from any central office in which the manager and/or employees require privacy to determine procedures.
>
> 8. If you read or see on television any report concerning the company, the community and its employees or residents, it would be helpful if you notified the office of _____ about this. Save clippings (full newspaper page) and videos, if possible.
>
> 9. Above all, employees should remember:
>   a. Whether in a crisis situation or not, YOU ARE NEVER REQUIRED TO TALK TO THE PRESS, even if they have identified themselves to you. You are not violating any law by refusing to speak to any media representative.
>   b. Unscrupulous people use the forged press cards and ID's to gain entry. Be wise and check with a superior before supplying any information to anyone identifying themselves as "the press" or "with the press."
>
> 10. In all cases, if you are unsure what you should do, courteously tell your media caller you will be glad to "get back to them" with the answer. Take their name and number. Then call the office of _____ for guidance.

Create Effective Press Releases

Press releases can be used to convey newsworthy information. Basically, a press release should answer the "Ws" (who, what, where, when, and why) and "H" (how). A good press release is short and communicates facts without exaggeration or excessive adjectives. It follows an inverted pyramid with the most important information in the first paragraph followed by other details in descending order of importance. Many newspapers offer news coverage tips and these should be read and practiced, as well.

Figure 12-2. Sample press release: seminar series.

Note: This gives an example of a press release; topics included are suggestions and are included for format purposes only.

<u>FOR IMMEDIATE RELEASE</u>

DATE: _____

CONTACT: _____

PHONE: _____

Announcing: "By Invitation Only" . . . A Seminar Series Debuting at COMMUNITY in MONTH.

CITY – "By Invitation Only," a special series of seminars ranging from health and legal topics to graphology and the theater, will debut in COMMUNITY, a new luxury senior retirement community located off LOCATION.

The first afternoon program highlighting TOPIC will be held on DAY, DATE, at 3:00 p.m. in the visitor area of COMMUNITY Information Center at ADDRESS. Admission is free but seating is limited and advance reservations are required. Information on the weekly program series is available by calling TELEPHONE NUMBER.

Each program will begin at three o-clock on DAY, for approximately 30 to 45 minutes, followed by a question and answer session and light refreshments when guests will have the opportunity to meet the speakers personally.

The seminar will open DATE with DESCRIPTION OF PROGRAM/SPEAKER AND NAME OF SPEAKER, discussing DESCRIPTION OF PROGRAM (e.g., care of the eyes and what to expect from examinations, as well as the newest techniques to preserve eyesight).

Subsequent programs will include DESCRIPTION OF PROGRAMS.

"We are offering these weekly programs as a public service and as a way of showing how retirement communities can positively influence better health care and encourage more positive living," commented NAME, Project Director for COMMUNITY.

"Many of the programs we are presenting will parallel the activities and events which will take place the year-around at COMMUNITY Community Center," NAME said. "Thus our residents and guests can sample some of the informative and cultural programming we plan for the community in advance."

The Community Center at COMMUNITY, a # sq. ft. building, is connected directly to apartment residential buildings and will include casual and formal dining areas, a convenience store, barber-beauty salon, activity center, recreational facilities and a Wellness Center.

Figure 12-3. Sample calendar notice.

SEMINAR PROGRAMS: MONTH, YEAR

Note: The time for all programs listed is 3:00 p.m.

Date	Title/Speaker/Description
DATE	"Your Eyes & Your Health," by Dr. NAME, optometrist. Eye care; what to expect from examinations; new techniques in eyesight preservation.
DATE	"Understanding & Preventing Strokes," by Dr. NAME, neurologist. Description of stroke process; diet and exercise advice to reduce likelihood of strokes.
DATE	"Planning Your Florida Estate," by NAME, attorney. Updating Florida estate and tax planning; conservation methods.

Planned for MONTH – A visit from NAME, Producing Director of the THEATER NAME on DATE; Dr. NAME describes causes and treatments of sleeping disorders on DATE; "Echoes of the Mind," a provocative look at handwriting traits and analysis by graphology specialist NAME on DATE.

For guests: Convenient parking is available immediately adjacent to COMMUNITY Information Center. Directions: Take …. [Community Name] will be on your [right/left] side.

Figure 12-4. Sample press release: individual program.

Note: Print media must be sent at least two weeks in advance of the event.

TO: Calendar Editor (or Name of Editor) CONTACT: _____
   (Name of News Media Publication) TELEPHONE: ____
RE: Free Seminar/Open to Public
   (Day), (Date), 3:00 p.m.: "Your Eyes & Your Health"
Dr. NAME, optometrist, presents a free seminar on eye care, designed for adult retirees in the "By Invitation Only" series at COMMUNITY Information Center, ADDRESS. Light refreshments follow program. Advance reservations required; TELEPHONE NUMBER for additional information.

Generally only one person is quoted in a press release and, therefore, it is not a group collaboration quoting an executive manager, director of sales, and others.

Directing a press release to the correct person at the news publication requires skill and intuition as well as knowledge of the newspaper. Don't send a press release to someone without first checking either a hard copy of the paper or an online version to identify reporters who cover a specific topic.

Usually press releases are distributed via E-mail rather than fax or mail. Be sure to allow adequate time for a reporter to cover your news. You may need to follow-up with additional E-mails, but be careful not to overload a reporter with too many requests. If you are trying to achieve coverage, there are only so many times you can go to the same reporters. It is better not to be greedy.

Your Publicity Plan

A publicity plan should encompass at least six months and should be updated monthly as new information becomes available. Plan in advance the topics on which you will focus.

Suggested topics include:

- Events – What will be happening at the community and does the event warrant coverage? Is the event open to the public or is it a resident-only event?
- Community updates – What is programmed for this period regarding construction, renovation, new programs, menu changes, equipment installations, and so on?
- Activity programming – Are there new classes being introduced or is something different being undertaken by residents?
- Special celebrations – Is the community doing something special for the holidays?
- Special events – Is the community doing anything different with regards to special events, inter-generational programs, or educational offerings?
- Staff announcements – What staff positions can be publicized as new-hires join the community?
- Awards and recognition – Have the community, staff, or residents received any awards or recognitions recently that could be announced?

Press/Media Kits

It is good to be prepared for media requests with a media kit. While it may sound foreboding, it really is somewhat simple to compile. A media kit can include:

- Kit cover/folder
- Short bios/backgrounds of key staff with headshot pictures

- If community is under construction: renderings and background of development team
- If community is open: exterior/interior pictures
- Background press release conveying factual information about the community that could be used in its entirety
- Community fact sheet
- Relevant material for a specific event (such as a bio sheet for the speaker, an agenda, or talking points)
- Glossary/terminology of the senior housing industry (which could help a reporter)
- Community brochure or address for web site
- Reprints of releases

What Can We Write About?

There is a wealth that can be written about a community and senior management can be publicized as experts for the industry. When a community becomes home for residents, they also offer rich opportunities for coverage

It takes "a nose for news." An activity calendar may show activities that will be pleasing to residents, but are far from newsworthy. A picture of a room full of residents sitting and listening to a speaker is not as captivating as a picture of a youngster holding his or her pet for a senior to stroke during an inter-generational event.

When determining what to write, consider the following:
- Community goals and timeframes of significant events
- Market trends for senior housing
- History of the community
- Leasing/sales history
- Reputation of community and owner/management
- Achievements of community/company ownership
- Residents' input
- Memberships/affiliations that community supports
- Participation in local/national trade shows
- Pricing and comparison to other communities
- Community's strengths and weaknesses
- Advertising (what is being spent and where)
- How prospective inquiries are handled

- Current marketing issues and challenges
- Press clippings and notable press coverage

Publicity Ideas

New Community
- Groundbreaking
- Community goals for development/leasing
- Market trends and why company selected this site/city
- Construction updates
- Key personnel hires
- Grand opening

Established Community
- Residents who volunteer
- Notable residents related to key holidays/subjects
- Innovative activities
- Open to the public events
- Community milestones
- Interesting employees

In Print or Not…It's Still Good PR

Congratulations if your press release is used by the media or generates press coverage, but it doesn't end there. Good coverage is worth its weight in gold and has long-lasting benefits as reprints and on the community's web site.

It is very limited exposure to frame an article for the CEO's office without taking advantage of merchandising opportunities and making everyone in the community aware of the article. Reprints are inexpensive and can be done either by staff or a local printing company. Their value is close to timeless because few people look at a reprint's date. Direct-mail the reprint to your lead base and referral sources with a note, "Thought you'd enjoy reading about our community." Posting the link to the newsroom on the community's web site is good, as well as including the article.

Crisis Public Relations

While there are books and specialists specific to this topic, it is very important to plan in advance for not only the handling of a crisis, but also how it will be addressed with the media. Make no mistake— the press covers crisis situations. In senior communities these crises may range from a flu epidemic to a deer walking through the front door. You are in a "people business" and crises can involve employees and residents as well as natural disasters. How a crisis is handled may reverberate for years. It is far better to be prepared with a plan that is periodically reviewed with team members than to attempt to react without a plan.

Figure 12-5. Project fact sheet checklist.

FACT SHEET: _____

                  (Name of Community)

ADDRESS: _____

                  (Street Address)

                  (City of Unincorporated County) (State)

TEL/FAX: _____

                  (Project Office Tel.) (Project Office Fax)

DESCRIPTION: _____

                  (Number of units)

                  (Site size)

                  (Special site features)

                  (Facilities: clubhouse, swimming pool, etc.)

                  (Amenities: lake/water views, parks, etc.)

PROJECT COST: _____

                  ($ Estimate)

CONFIGUR'N: No. Bldgs.____ No. Stories: ____No. Units____

CONFIGUR'N:
(List by no. of
BR/BA and ea.
sq. ft.)

_____
_____
_____
_____

From $ _____ to $ _____

RENTAL RANGE: _____

UNIT FEATURES: _____
(List: Central
AC/Heat, Kitchen   _____
Equip., Tiling, etc.)   _____

PARTICIPATING   _____
AGENCIES:

(List gov't supporting groups, local/county)

_____
_____

PROJECT   Groundbreaking:
SCHEDULE:
(Use Target Dates,   _____
Month/Year)   Pre-Leasing:

_____

Completion:

_____

PROJECT
MANAGEMENT: _____

PROJECT
ARCHITECT: _____

PROJECT
DEVELOPER: _____

PROJECT
CONTRACTOR: _____

PROJECT
CONTACT: _____

(Name/Title)   (Tel.)

ADDITIONAL   _____
DETAIL (Use this
space & continue on _____
reverse to include   _____
other details.)   _____

Figure 12-6. Fact sheet form.

_____ : *Project Fact Sheet*

1. General Information

Street Address_____City _____ZIP _____
Mailing Address_____City _____ZIP _____
Sales Ctr Address _____City _____ZIP _____
Tel._____ Fax _____E-mail _____
Location Boundaries: North _____
Site Acres(s)/Sq Ft   South _____
_____ /_____   East _____
                            West _____

Total Units	Phase I Buildings/ Residences	Phase II Buildings/ Residences	Total Buildings/ Residences
1. Villas	____ /____	____ /____	____ /____
2. Town	____ /____	____ /____	____ /____
3. S/F Homes	____ /____	____ /____	____ /____
4. Condo/Apts	____ /____	____ /____	____ /____
5. Other	____ /____	____ /____	____ /____
Totals	____ /____	____ /____	____ /____

Major Facilities ( ) Community Ctr   Sq Ft_____ Stories ____
                    ( ) Restaurant   " _____
                    ( ) Recreational Area   " _____
                    ( ) Golf Course   Length ____ Club _____
                    ( ) Tennis Court(s)   No. Cts. ___ Club _____
                    ( ) Swimming Pool(s)   Sq Ft_____ Club _____
Other   ( ) _____
                    ( ) _____
                    ( ) _____
                    ( ) _____

2. Community

Development   _____
Company   (Name)   (City)   (State)

Contact Name   _____

                     (Name)   (Title)   (Tel.)

Other Communities _____

Built/Managed   _____

                         _____

New Community   _____

Concept   _____

                         _____

Resident Profile   _____

                         _____

                         _____

Income Range $_____ to $ _____

Financing Plan   _____

                         _____

                         _____

Management   _____

Company   (Name)   (City)   (State)

Contact Name   _____

                     (Name)   (Title)   (Tel.)

Resident Cost		***Single/Couple***
Independent Living	Monthly Minimal	Cost ___ /___
		to Maximum ___ /___
Assisted Living	Monthly Minimal	Cost ___ /___
		to Maximum ___ /___
Skilled NF	Daily Minimal	Cost ___ /___
		to Maximum ___ /___
Primary Benefits		_____

_____

_____

3. Product Details

Residences	Villas ( )	( ) Towns	( ) Apts	( ) Other
Model Name/#	_____	_____	_____	_____
	__BR__BA	__BR__BA	__BR__BA	__BR__BA
	____ sq ft	____ sq ft	____ sq ft	____ sq ft
Model Name/#	_____	_____	_____	_____
	__BR__BA	__BR__BA	__BR__BA	__BR__BA
	____ sq ft	____ sq ft	____ sq ft	____ sq ft
Model Name/#	_____	_____	_____	_____
	__BR__BA	__BR__BA	__BR__BA	__BR__BA
	____ sq ft	____ sq ft	____ sq ft	____ sq ft
Model Name/#	_____	_____	_____	_____
	__BR__BA	__BR__BA	__BR__BA	__BR__BA
	____ sq ft	____ sq ft	____ sq ft	____ sq ft
Model Name/#	_____	_____	_____	_____
	__BR__BA	__BR__BA	__BR__BA	__BR__BA
	____ sq ft	____ sq ft	____ sq ft	____ sq ft
Model Name/#	_____	_____	_____	_____
	__BR__BA	__BR__BA	__BR__BA	__BR__BA
	____ sq ft	____ sq ft	____ sq ft	____ sq ft
Price Range From:	$_____	$_____	$_____	$_____
Price Range To:	$_____	$_____	$_____	$_____
Standard Features (Key Sales Points)	_____	_____	_____	_____
	_____	_____	_____	_____
	_____	_____	_____	_____
	_____	_____	_____	_____
	_____	_____	_____	_____
	_____	_____	_____	_____
	_____	_____	_____	_____
	_____	_____	_____	_____
Optional Features (List Major)	_____	_____	_____	_____
	_____	_____	_____	_____
	_____	_____	_____	_____

4. Service Areas

Check All Applicable Boxes				Basic Plan	Optional Cost
( ) On-site Dining	( ) Breakfast	( ) Lunch	( ) Dinner	( )	( )
( ) On-site Store	( ) Daily	( ) Nightly	( ) Sat/Sun	( )	( )
( ) On-site Wellness	( ) Daily	( ) Nightly	( ) 24-Hour	( )	( )
( ) On-site Security	( ) Daily	( ) Nightly	( ) 24-Hour	( )	( )
( ) On-site Concierge	( ) Daily	( ) Nightly	( ) 24-Hour	( )	( )
( ) On-site Salon	( ) Daily	( ) Sat/Sun	( ) By Appt	( )	( )
( ) Bus Transportation	( ) Daily	( ) Nightly	( ) Sat/Sun	( )	( )
( ) Van Transportation	( ) Daily	( ) Nightly	( ) Sat/Sun	( )	( )
( ) Limo Transportation	( ) Daily	( ) Nightly	( ) Sat/Sun	( )	( )
( ) Mail/Cleaning	( ) Daily	( ) Weekly	( ) Monthly	( )	( )
( ) Maintenance	( ) Daily	( ) Weekly	( ) Monthly	( )	( )

Other _____

_____

Additional Services (list all)	Circle Applicable Days							Basic Plan	Optional Cost
( ) Banking	( ) Daily	M	T	W	Th	F	S/S	( )	( )
( )	( ) Daily	M	T	W	Th	F	S/S	( )	( )
( )	( ) Daily	M	T	W	Th	F	S/S	( )	( )
( )	( ) Daily	M	T	W	Th	F	S/S	( )	( )
( )	( ) Daily	M	T	W	Th	F	S/S	( )	( )
( )	( ) Daily	M	T	W	Th	F	S/S	( )	( )

5. Primary Activities (Check as applicable)

( ) Activity Director	( ) Part-Time	( ) Full-Time	( ) Evenings/Weekends
( ) Theater	( ) Movies	( ) Live Shows	( ) Other _____
( ) Physical Fitness	( ) Daily	( ) Appt Only	( ) Classes_____
( ) Card Room	( ) Daily	( ) Tournaments	( ) Other_____
( ) Billiards Room	( ) Daily	( ) Evenings	( ) Weekends
( ) Swimming	( ) Daily	( ) Instructor	( ) Weekends
( ) Library	( ) Daily	( ) Loan Outs	( ) Weekends
( ) Arts/Crafts	( ) Daily	( ) Instructor	( ) Classes

Additional Activities   Comment: _____

6. Sales Center

Location _____

            (Address)   (City)   (State)   (ZIP)

Mailing Address (if different) _____

_____

Sales Tel. _____ Fax _____ E-mail _____

Hours: Weekday_____ to _____ Sat/Sun _____to _____

Directional _____

_____

_____

Sales Director _____

Sales Associates _____

_____

_____

Describe Center _____

_____

_____

           Overall Sq Ft _____

Model Name(s) _____ _____ _____

Model Location(s) _____ _____ _____

Model Décor by _____ Tel. _____

Community Interiors by _____ Tel. _____

No. of Elevations ___ Architect _____ Tel. _____

Parking Area   Overall Sq Ft _____

           No. Guest Spots _____

7. Development Principals

Development Entity _____

	Principal/Company	Publish: Yes	No
Partnership(s)	_____	( )	( )
	_____	( )	( )
	Principal/Company		
Joint Venture w/	_____	( )	( )
	_____	( )	( )
	Principal/Company		
Permanent Financing by_____ Date Secured _____		( )	( )

Amount $_____ ( ) ( )
Construction Loan by _____ Date Secured _____ ( ) ( )
Amount $_____ ( ) ( )
Financial/CPA _____ Tel. _____
Legal/Attorneys _____ Tel. _____
Land Plan/Engineer _____ Tel. _____
Architect _____ Tel. _____
Landscaping_____ Tel. _____
Interiors _____ Tel. _____
Other_____ Tel. _____
General Contractor _____ Tel. _____
On-Site Address_____ Tel. _____
Spokesperson/Title_____ Tel. _____
Subcontractors _____ For _____ Tel. _____
_____ For _____ Tel. _____
_____ For _____ Tel. _____

Figure 12-7. Biographical data form.
Name (full): _____
In what city/state do you live: _____
Employed by: _____
Full job title: _____
Gen'l job description: _____

Education (if you earned a degree, what degree and from what
institution/location):

Prior employment/experience (background that qualifies you for
position – if you have a resume, please supply; if not, jot down prior
career experience):
Employer ____ Title _____ Location____ Responsibilities___

_____   _____   _____

_____   _____   _____

Licenses: _____

Professional memberships: _____

Community/civic organizations (serve on any boards): _____

Charitable organizations/interests: _____

Recent awards/recognition:_____

Personal hobbies/interests: _____

Where were you born (if outside of Florida, when did you relocate):

_____

What do you feel are your biggest strengths: _____

Spouse's name: _____
Children's names & ages: _____

Chapter 13:

||||||||||||||||||||||||||||||||||||||||||||||||||||||||||||||||||||||||||||||||||||||||||||||||||||||||||||||||||||

Creative Promotional Events —
A Sure Path to Prospects

Using creative promotional events to generate and sustain interest among potential residents of your community is a marketing tactic guaranteed to pay big dividends.

Events are very helpful to build interest during a community's initial marketing efforts and their value continues as the community matures. During lease-up or pre-sales, events can publicize the community's name, build a list of prospects, and create goodwill. Down the line, events excite prospects and keep them enthusiastic; build on the tradition and reputation you are establishing; and help set your community apart from the competition. There will always be apartments to fill and events help in creating the continual interest needed to bring new traffic to the door.

Even when events are not open to the public (for example, are limited to residents or prospects only), they can be vehicles for publicity. Taking an event and spinning it to create media interest may be an opportunity waiting to be explored. For example, a community was going to install a new flagpole and American flag without any fanfare. This became a PR dream. After brainstorming between the activity director and PR person, what was a seemingly insignificant event made the evening news. The event evolved to include a high school band, Eagle Scouts, military veterans, and speeches from the city's mayor and corporate executives. "Let's put up a flagpole" became the lead story on TV and the front page of the newspaper with a caption that mentioned the community. Residents were pleased to live somewhere so significant and prospective residents were reminded that this community was special.

Making Events Work for You

In building name awareness, less is *not* more. But events just for events' sake require unnecessary expense. An event needs to have a clear purpose.

The number of events that a staff can handle is an important consideration. If a weekend event is planned, this may require overtime for employees and additional staff. If an event is planned in the evening, care needs to be taken to not infringe on residents.

Feasible budgeting is important, too. How much should be allocated to events? You need to spend enough to put your best foot forward. This can entail seasonal decorations, picnic lunches with music and clowns, or elaborate cocktail parties and black tie affairs. Always remember that events need to be tailored to suit your potential residents and audiences. Creativity and event planning go hand in hand. A good test of an event's potential appeal is to ask yourself "Would I attend this event?" If the answer is no, then why do you think your prospective residents or referral sources would find it intriguing?

Figure 13-1. Promotional event checklist, sample #1.

Promotional Event Checklist:
Title of Event: _____

Event Host: _____

_____

Date: _____
Start by (time): _____Finish by (time): _____
Location: _____
Address/Directions: _____

_____

Contact/Phone (at the location): _____
Contact Person/Phone (for RSVP): _____
Description of Event: _____

_____

Prepare/Design Guest Invitation: _____

Budget for Invitation Design/Printing: $ _____

Number of Invitations Printed:_____

Number of Guests to be Invited: _____

Guest RSVP Date/Contact (phone number): _____

Prepare Guest/Mailing List: _____

Address Invitations/Mailing: _____

Emcee: _____

Speakers: _____

Special Guests: _____

_____

Guest Registration Table (man the table):_____

Name Tags (prepare): _____

Event Agenda (prepare & prep speakers): _____

Will Food be Served: _____

Refreshments (or) Full Meal: _____Budget: $ _____

Caterer: _____

Menu Basics: _____

_____

_____

Rental Company: _____

Rental Items (tent/tables/chairs/linens): _____

Florist: _____

Decorations (balloons):_____

Centerpieces (for tables):_____

Special Equipment Needed (microphone, speakers, podium, etc.):

_____

Set-Up Time/Personnel: _____

_____

Clean-Up Time/Personnel:_____

_____

Event Guest Program (author/design): _____

Event Guest Program (budget): $ _____

Event Guest Program (number to be printed): _____

Commemorative Give-Away (speakers): _____

Commemorative Give-Away (budget): _____

Commemorative Give-Away (quantity): _____

Guest Give-Away:_____

Guest Give-Away (budget): $ ___ Guest Give-Away (quantity): __

Give-Away Distribution:_____

On-Site Commemorative Plaque: _____

Misc./Notes:_____

_____

_____

_____

_____

_____

_____

Figure 13-2. Promotional event checklist, sample #2.

Community: _____Date: _____

Location: _____Time: _____

Invitation: _____Date to be mailed: _____

Staff to address envelopes: _____

Staff to handle RSVPs:_____

Follow-up RSVP: _____

Caterer - name & phone: _____

Food/menu: _____

Bar: _____

Check requests: _____

Confirmation letter(s) to speaker: _____

Special equipment: _____

Electrical requirements: _____

Rentals: _____

Set-up: _____Clean-up: _____

Photographer:_____

Name tags/pens:_____Give-a-way: _____

Traffic requirements: _____

Flowers: _____Trash cans/bags:_____

Staff members: _____

Person to introduce speaker:_____

Notify Maintenance: _____Notify Leasing: _____

Other: _____

What Kinds of Events Should We Hold?

Know who you want to reach and attract to an event. This helps tailor the event to fit different groups of people—prospects, referral sources, and, of course, residents.

Emphasizing community events that counter the "old folks' home" stereotype and show seniors in a positive light is a no-fail approach to creating new traffic and referrals.

Figure 13-3. Sample promotional event invitation.

Get the information you need before deciding.
Four things you can do today!
Check all that apply – and mail today (the postage is paid)

☐ Invite me to future seminars and special events.

☐ Learn more about the 90% refundable investment option.

☐ Send me The Mather's information package immediately.

☐ E-mail me a copy of Chef Chip's award-winning chocolate banana creme brûlée French Toast recipe.

First Name _____
Last Name _____
Address _____
City _____ Street _____ Zip _____
Phone _____
E-mail _____

Mather de Mayo
Wednesday, May 5

Let's invent new holidays

The Mather Evanston, IL

Get ready...
for a taste of The Mather!

You're invited to toast Mather de Mayo, a holiday that celebrates cutting loose from convention and discovering The Mather, Evanston's newest choice for senior living. While enjoying festive appetizers, desserts, and beverages, learn more about our seven dining* and lounge venues, 10,000 square-foot fitness center and spa, our convenient location just steps from downtown Evanston, and why so many people just like you are throwing their hats in The Mather ring! ¡Olé!

425 Davis Street, Evanston, IL 60201

Mather de Mayo

When: Wednesday, May 5 at 2 p.m.

Where: The Mather
425 Davis Street
Evanston, IL 60201

Complementary Valet Parking is located at the Davis Street entrance.

Please RSVP by Monday, May 3 at (847) 448.0793

*All of our dining venues are under the direction of Executive Chef Chip Ferport, winner of the young professional "Sous Chef" style competition for chefs from across the country sponsored by the American Association of Homes and Services for the Aged.

www.themathervanston.com • e-mail: themather@matherlifeways.com

BUSINESS REPLY MAIL
FIRST CLASS   MAIL PERMIT 1749   EVANSTON, IL

POSTAGE WILL BE PAID BY ADDRESSEE

Mather LifeWays
Attn: The Mather
1603 Orrington Avenue, Suite 1800
Evanston, IL 60201-9886

NO POSTAGE
NECESSARY
IF MAILED
IN THE
UNITED STATES

Source: Mather LifeWays, Evanston, Illinois

Referral Source Events

Every senior community should consider building referral sources from within the local area. From doctors, hospital discharge coordinators, social workers, and clergy to estate attorneys and guardians, these potential sources need an event with special *oomph* to grab their attention. (Unfortunately there is never a guarantee that invited guests will come. Based on experience, the likelihood that those in the medical field will find their way to your door is generally low.)

An eye-catching invitation tied to an equally appealing event certainly puts out a great message. Success cannot always be measured merely by attendance; having the invitation read is of value, too.

Event Benefits

The benefits of an event include the following:

- Building name awareness (especially helpful with potential referral sources)
- Acquainting seminar presenters with the community
- Forging a positive identity for the community
- Projecting a good citizen image by offering no-cost educational and social opportunities
- Offering a "be-back" visit to which leasing counselors can extend invitations
- Increasing exposure for the community's name
- Offering community updates
- Building prospect lists
- Expanding and educating potential referral sources
- Creating opportunities for pre-and post-event publicity as another way to get the community's name in the news

A side benefit of great events is that they offer residents interesting content to share with their children in relating what they did that day. It's like sending your child to camp or college and having them share their experiences. Events that are distinctive and stimulating reap far more rewards than may initially be recognized.

Event Photography

So much time and energy is expended in creating and managing events that photography is often overlooked or delegated to a staff person working the event. While many things can be recreated, an event often cannot. Using professional photographers to capture events may be well worth the expense. The resulting photos are useful in newsletters, web sites, press releases, and when given to residents.

Topical Seminars

Many senior housing marketers focus on seminars as a way to toot their horn, explaining why someone should move to the community. These are often educational programs explaining senior housing options. In geographic areas that are not already inundated with senior living communities, this topic may be especially worthwhile. Other topical seminars that are entertaining, motivating, educational, and even humorous send a message to prospects that this is a community with stimulating and interesting activities.

Seniors considering your community are making a market-based, need-driven decision. Educational or motivational seminars can be a less-threatening, more-enticing way to bring prospects to the door. They know they can look you over informally and perhaps bring a family member without the pressure to make a commitment then and there. Let's face it—an over-exuberant or aggressive salesperson extolling the virtues of a community may be less appealing than a concert or lecture.

Program Suggestions	
Topic	Speaker
Downsizing, moving	Specialist in topic
New artists on the cultural scene	Gallery owner, museum curator
Healthy eating (eat this, not that)	Nutritionist
New design trends	Architect, interior designer
History of local area	Historian, architect
Seniors and fraud	Police, FBI, Post Office personnel

Notice that in these program suggestions, you may find at least a few topics of personal interest ("Would I attend this event?"). Remember, this is the key question to assess topics.

Scheduling Options

An ongoing series of seminars is a good approach. Programs are typically held weekly or twice monthly, preferably on a mid-week afternoon. Or if the event is geared to families, scheduling on weekends—especially on Sunday afternoons—makes sense.

Events held shortly after a community opens can be ideal for new residents to invite their friends; they'll enjoy showing off the community and their new home.

In time, as a community approaches fuller occupancy, the events can be phased into the overall activities program with an active director planning which events can be open to the public and/or lead base.

Youth and Intergenerational Programs

Youth programs can be of value if you avoid the nursing home connotations. Youth events need to be of interest to both the youngsters and seniors. Creativity is key.

Establishing relationships with local public and/or private schools offers many possibilities. When you link you own programs and recruit teen involvement, you are offering opportunity for volunteerism—an important part of college applications.

Senior proms and back-to-school visits are wonderful ways to provide interactions between residents and teens. So is a pet day when students bring dogs, cats, birds, and other home pets to share with seniors.

In the new world of social media, maybe some "techie" students want to come and talk about how to use Facebook and Twitter to connect with grandchildren.

ABCs of a Speaker's Series

When developing a speaker's series, forward planning is essential. You need to allow sufficient time to publicize the event and coordinate all the logistics. To create a successful program, allow four to six weeks to produce and mail invitations, place advertising, and publicize your event.

Planning for groups of three to six seminars is sometimes easier than planning only one. Identifying suitable topics and speakers are the first challenges to tackle. Once the speaker is booked, the rest seems to fall into place.

Figure 13-4. Sample information seminar series invitation.

Are you open...to the possibilities?

The Mather is a continuing care retirement community and a forward-thinking destination for those who've always planned ahead. We offer you a variety of long-term assurances that provide both financial and personal peace of mind, including:

• Investment protection – a 90% refundable investment that will always be there, guaranteed
• Predictable costs
• Life care options that allow you to meet all your health care needs
• Prime location in the heart of Evanston within walking distance to everything

 Please R.S.V.P. for one or all of the Repriorment 101 Sessions by calling (847) 859.9918 or e-mailing themather@matherlifeways.com

425 Davis Street Evanston Illinois 60201

Repriorment 101

Repriorment means discovering the joy of new directions and rethinking your shelved but not forgotten priorities, passions, and dreams. Something you *want* to do – not have to do. Instead of narrowing your outlook, why not expand it?

Hear all about Repriorment from our experts and residents at The Mather.

When: March 10: Is Repriorment right for me? at 10:00 a.m.

March 24: What is a Continuing Care Retirement Community? at 10:00 a.m.

April 7: Culinary Delights at 11:30 a.m.

Where: The Mather
425 Davis Street
Evanston, IL 60201

Please R.S.V.P. for one or all of the Repriorment 101 Sessions by calling (847) 859.9918 or e-mailing themather@matherlifeways.com

 www.thematherevanston.com • e–mail:themather@matherlifeways.com

Repriorment 101
at The Mather

A new state of mind
brought to you by
The Mather

Information Seminar Series:
Repriorment 101 – Wednesdays, March 10, March 24, and April 7

The Mather Evanston, IL

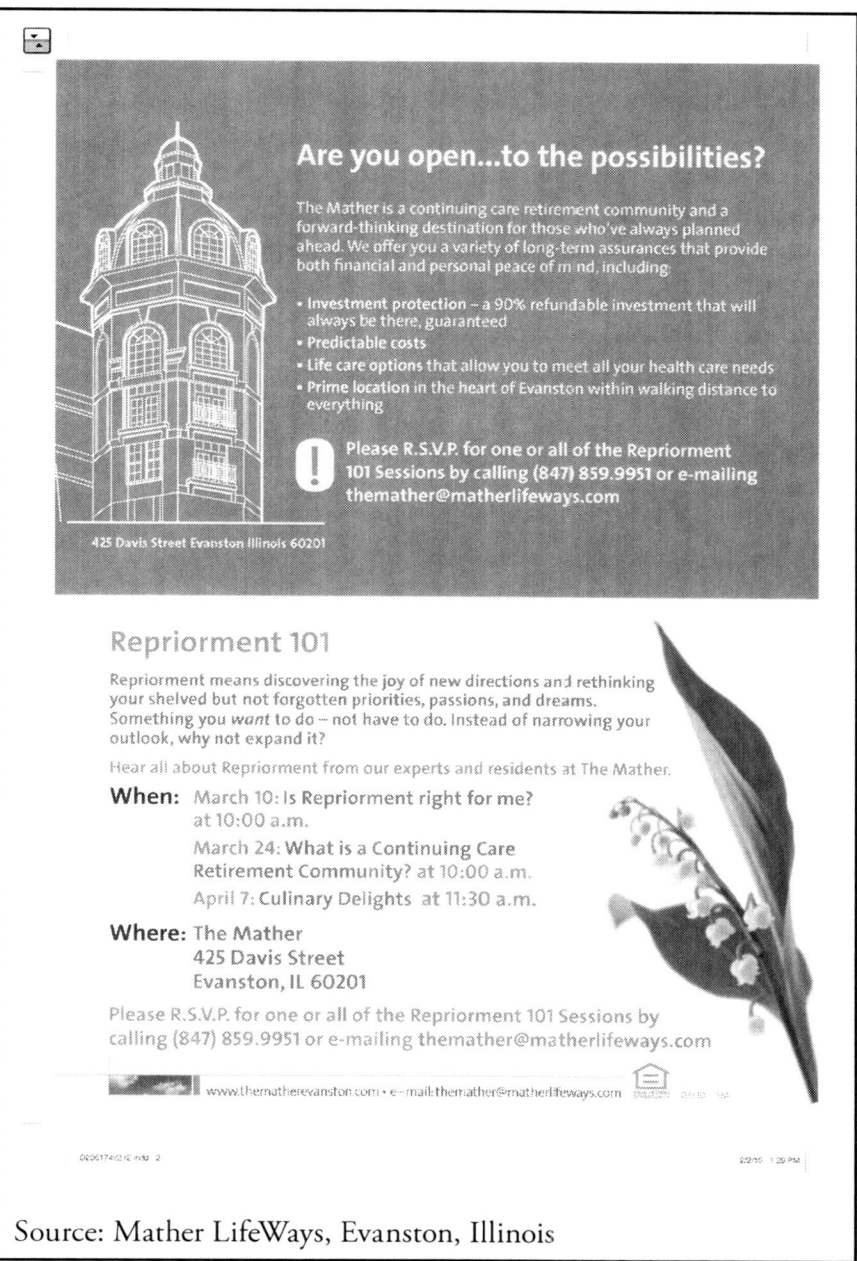

Source: Mather LifeWays, Evanston, Illinois

In some cities a speaker's bureau may be a resource. It may take some ferreting out, but speakers can be found through museums and cultural organizations, universities, government, and business. A gerontologist may be willing to speak on new findings in aging, while a clergy member may narrate a slide show of a recent trip to the Holy Land. A retiree may recount adventures as an intelligence officer during the war. The possibilities are limited only by your creativity. (We found a retired Jewish rabbi who had marched with Martin Luther King, Jr., and he was an inspired speaker.) Work with the local Chamber of Commerce and service organizations such as Rotary Club or Kiwanis Club for liaisons to key professionals and nonprofit organizations.

Figure 13-5. Local resources for speakers.

Hospital
Chamber of Commerce
Public library
Cultural facilities in the area:
    Orchestra, museums, theaters
Local media:
    Newspaper, radio, television
    Reporters, editors, station managers
Police department
Fire department/emergency medical services
Project interior designer
Local colleges
Local, city, and county government
Local authors
Health-related associations

After you have identified the speaker, confirm the engagement in writing. Include a community brochure and other pertinent information to familiarize the speaker with the audience. Do a telephone confirmation two weeks prior and again the week of the event to minimize the possibility of a no-show speaker. (Unfortunately, it happens.)

Giving the speaker a certificate of appreciation at the end of the presentation is a nice touch, or give a memento of the occasion. Follow up with thank-you letters to the speaker and all guests.

Tip: Include RSVPs in the press release and invitations to control the number of people attending and help plan seating. If people who did not make reservations attend and seating is limited, you may need to politely ask them to wait until reservations are honored.

Measuring Event Success

Conventional wisdom may say that events are successful when all the chairs are filled and the parking lot is overflowing. Others may weigh success on the number of deals made the day of the event. Yet even events that produce only a handful of people can be worthwhile. The so-called "failed event" still got your name in someone's mailbox. It may have piqued the interest of a solid prospect. And while someone may not have attended the event, it still illustrated that this is a "happening community."

It is difficult to gauge the effectiveness of a given event in terms of its costs and number of seats that were filled. Similarly looking at a promotional event only in terms of the number of deals written, and equating these deals to success, is shortsighted. Events provide so many ripple-effect benefits in public relations and name recognition that measuring their success is more subjective than objective.

Promotional events offer another side benefit; they spark internal enthusiasm. Staff can focus on something that's exciting and residents thrive on this infusion of revitalized energy. Just convene your team for event brainstorming and watch how quickly the focus goes to party planning.

Chapter 14:

||||||||||||||||||||||||||||||||||||||||||||||||||||||||||||||||||||||||||||||||||||||||||||||||||||||||

Who Leads Them to Your Door? – Spreading the Word for Referrals

Historically a marketing budget that includes consistent advertising is wonderful for those who can allocate funds to print and other media. Advertising creates name visibility. Size and frequency are integral. When budgets are cut or communities have a small allocation for print advertising, marketing staff may find itself relying on smaller ads while the competition, with bigger budgets, makes greater impact with larger, more frequent ads.

There are effective alternatives to a generous media budget. A vital source of customers is word-of-mouth advertising. In the senior housing industry, it is the best form of advertising.

If the community is in a pre-leasing or pre-sales period, word-of-mouth advertising must be tackled aggressively by outreach and networking because no one knows your name yet. Getting the buzz started there takes a commitment.

Later in a community's life, there are more spheres of influencers to tell your community's story and share it with others. Think about it. Why do your friends call to ask your advice on communities for their parents? For the same reason I ask my physician for the name of a dentist or I ask my family accountant for the name of an estate planning attorney. These referrals are much more valuable than a leads group passing out business cards without regard to the expertise and ability of its members or referral contacts.

A long-time senior housing owner-operator in South Florida knows that, when he and his wife attend a cocktail party, someone inevitably will ask his advice concerning an elderly parent. His name is long associated with providing good care for senior residents through his work in the industry. Getting your name known by the public is one of the most challenging marketing techniques because success is measured by time. When people start saying that they've heard of your community, you know you are getting your name out there.

Audits – A Starting Ground

A community audit is most helpful in determining the success of your outreach program as well as how you are perceived. Community audits are best undertaken by outside sources where biases can be eliminated. Various professionals and community resources are contacted for their input and, if they know of your community, what they think of it and what they hear about its reputation. One-on-one contact is made with potential referral sources like doctors, geriatric case managers, community activists, and community society leaders. You'd be surprised what you can learn by asking if someone has heard about your community.

It's worth asking the media, too. Have they heard of your community and what do they know about it?

In the case of senior housing, some people may not know about the community because there is not a personal interest or need. But when you learn that few have heard of your community or have no idea what it is about, you know what you need to work on.

Effectively reaching the leaders in the community takes more than a phone call or letter. You need to support their causes, be seen by them, and have them know your name. The executive director that doesn't encourage each and every person on his or her staff to get involved in the community in some way is very short-sighted.

Brainstorm a list of the senior resources in the community that you need to liaison with, and create a database of these contacts. Including the community's competitors is worthwhile, as well, because they also can refer potential residents.

"Out of sight, out of mind" certainly holds true when it comes to building a referral base.

Ambassadors Help Spread the Word

How do you get referral sources to your door? Experience has shown that, despite communities desiring to bring physicians to the community, in many cities this is an uphill battle. The typical cocktail party may not work in your city and it is fairly common that doctors will not attend.

What are alternatives? Create an Ambassador Program. What are Ambassadors? These are people who will come and hear about your community and then help spread the word. You may call them Ambassadors or advisors. They will help in telling your story.

By creating these referral groups, you can bridge the gap between the community at large and the retirement community. Depending on your community's size, these groups can form at a one-time meeting or meet on an on-going basis. Either way, the most important reasons for their existence are to bring people to your community, give you an opportunity to share your story, and then share it with others.

Figure 14-1. Sample Ambassador invitation flyer.

[Community Name]
Ambassadors Meeting
[Day], [Date] at [Time] [AM/PM]

[Community Name] Ambassadors are off to a great start, but we **still need help!** We need volunteers to help us spread the word about this special, new community in [City].

[Community Name] is a senior rental retirement community sponsored by the [City] Housing Authority. Opened this part January, [Community Name] is designed to meet the needs of the middle-income elderly citizens of [City]. [City] is one of the first cities to offer this type of senior living at an affordable rental price and yet [Community Name] remains a secret.

**Our [Community Name] Ambassadors
will help us open more doors,
make more contacts
and literally "spread the word"
about this special community**

Please join us for this one-hour meeting ...and bring a friend!

Meet the staff at [Community Name], hear the philosophies of the [City] Housing Authority, tour the community and enjoy a delicious Continental Breakfast!

Please call [Name], at [Community Name], and let us know if we can expect you: [Telephone Number]

[Community Name]
[Address]
[City, State, Zip Code]

Directions: Take .... [Community Name] will be on your [right/left] side.

For example, a nonprofit, independent living community was under-performing in its leasing program. The communications audit showed few key influencers in the city knew of the community. A local funeral home owner was invited to a breakfast and asked to be an Ambassador. He said that as soon as he became an Ambassador, he kept hearing positives about the community. Publicity received about the Ambassador Program also helped in name visibility. Before long, the community was receiving at least a referral a month.

Another example of success was inviting a Junior League member to an Ambassador breakfast. Following the meeting, she offered to E-mail a letter to her organization's members to tell them about the community. Needless to say, each of these Ambassadors was far more valuable than advertising. The cost of breakfast meetings paled in comparison to print advertising expenditures.

Ambassadors may also be cultivated with one-on-one meetings. Periodic visits to these potential referral resources can be planned for the executive director and/or marketing team.

Figure 14-2. Sample outreach letter for Ambassador use.

Dear _____,

[City] offers a unique living opportunity to its senior residents. We need your help to spread the word about this special community, [Community Name]. Perhaps you work closely with seniors or adults with elderly parents and you could tell them about this special community built to accommodate their needs.

[Community Name], sponsored by the [City] Housing Authority, is an innovative concept in the world of senior housing. [City] wants to reach out to its seniors and let them know there is a home for them here, an **affordable** one.

As people get older, their lifestyle and needs change. Owning a condo or a house with a yard is a lot of responsibility and work. Driving to the supermarket, the bank, or the doctor's office can become a hassle. Probably worst of all is the loneliness that so many seniors suffer from, not to mention that fact that money gets tight.

[Community Name] offers solutions to these common struggles for seniors. Opened for nearly a year, the apartments are brand new and spacious. Twenty-four-hour security offers comfort and every apartment has an emergency response system. Scheduled transportation is available to help residents get where they need to be.

The most important advantage for a senior at [Community Name] is the home-like atmosphere. Social activities are planned for residents. The dining room offers companionship at mealtime. There are attractively decorated lounge areas as well as craft, card, and TV rooms where residents can meet and share with friends and neighbors.

In addition to activities and friendly neighbors, [Community Name] offers another important amenity to its senior residents: independence. All apartments are fully equipped with kitchens and cable TV. Laundry facilities are located on each floor.

All services and utilities (except telephone) are included in one reasonable monthly fee, making bill-paying simple. [City] is offering to its seniors this unique opportunity that is too good to keep secret. [Community Name] wants to be a well-known and positive addition to the [City] community. Please keep us in mind and help us spread the word.

If you have any questions, please call us at [Telephone Number]. If you are interested in seeing [Community Name] we would be happy to give you a tour, just call to schedule an appointment.

Sincerely,

Additional Tips

Interfaith breakfasts are an excellent vehicle to invite clergy or provide a speaker from the community as a way to bring more people into the community.

One community has an annual luncheon for office managers in doctors' offices. They have recognized that it's not the doctor, but the office managers and nurses in the office with greater opportunities to talk with families and prospective residents. Their special event to reach this group is very enticing. Rather than host the event at the community, they select an upscale restaurant that is easily accessible. With a delicious menu and door prizes, the annual event has become a tradition.

Figure 14-3. Sample Ambassador letter to send to doctors.

Date Here

John Q. Physician, M.D.
XYZ Medical Group
1235 Royal Palm Way
City, State Zip

Dear Dr. XXXX:

You may not know about [Community Name], [City]'s newest senior rental retirement community. With the number of elderly patients you see, perhaps you may know of someone who could benefit from this special community setting.

[Community Name] is somewhat different from other rental communities because it is sponsored by the [City] Housing Authority and is geared to meet the needs of middle-income elderly citizens in our city. [Community Name] offers its residents studio, one- and two-bedroom apartments as well as daily social activities and services including transportation and two meals a day, all included in the monthly rental fee.

There are only 91 apartments at [Community Name] making it truly a family-oriented community. Our staff strives to treat each resident like a friend's mother or father. There is a sincere interest in the day-to-day well-being of every resident and communication with their families. Residents don't get lost in the shuffle at [Community Name].

[Community Name] is focused on elderly people who now face the challenges of living alone. Whether feeling sadness and depression that come from loneliness and worry, communities that offer residents a support system of friendship and emphasize group activities and social outlets are so valuable. These elements can truly impact one's outlook on life.

Enclosed is a copy of our community's brochure. We would be happy to welcome you or a staff member for a tour of [Community Name] and take the time to answer any questions you may have.

I look forward to being able to help you in serving those you may know who could benefit from [Community Name] and our special style of community living.

Warm regards,

[Name]
[Title]

Family members are a great referral source. Keep inviting them to community events as they welcome an opportunity to interact with their parents and have something of interest to share. And even when their parents are no longer residents, if they have had a good experience with your staff and your community, they'll continue to spread a good word.

It is very valuable to brainstorm with your staff about potential senior resources in your city. Knowing about the competition is very worthwhile. There may be times when someone does not fit your particular community. Whereas in new home sales you would never send someone down the street, helping a family by referring someone to another community is a goodwill gesture.

Gifts and Mementos

Who will say no to a thoughtful gift? Once referral sources have been identified, it is useful to drop off periodic mementoes as a way to keep your name front and center. These gifts can vary and range in creativity. From homemade pie, cookies, or soup from your community's kitchen to chocolates from a local candy store, these items are thoughtful and make a nice impression. Small, useful gifts also work well and, when combined in a gift bag, have multiple uses for outreach visitors to take home after a tour.

Exit Interviews

If someone vacates the community, calling these former residents and their families is a worthwhile gesture that is often overlooked. This is so valuable in building relationships for positive referrals. Called "exit interviews," these offer an opportunity for people to provide constructive advice about their experiences with the community. People rarely seem to mind sharing their insights when asked. Using an outside resource is important in conducting exit interviews rather than having staff from the community call former residents. It's important for people to feel they can share their thoughts without insulting or jeopardizing an employee.

Chapter 15:

||||||||||||||||||||||||||||||||||||||||||||||||||||||||||||||||||||||||||||||||||||||||||||||||||||||||

The Networking Connection – Creating and Using a Networking Plan for Outreach

The well-known line "Build it and they will come" from the movie *Field of Dreams* may apply to filling bleacher seats, but does not work with senior housing. It takes much more than a site sign to successfully lease or sell apartments.

Most people don't wake up one morning and think "This month I'll move to a senior community," and they aren't sitting and waiting for the telephone to ring with an invitation to change their life. Relocating is a major life decision and one that is typically given much consideration and study by potential residents and families.

Statistics vary but prospective residents may shop eight or more communities, visiting each four or more times. Their decision may be put on the back burner for later consideration but then become more relevant should a need arise that motivates their decision. While a health crisis or death of a spouse often motivate a move, rest assured— these folks have probably discussed this decision with their children and friends. Doctors, attorneys, CPAs, and clergy may be solicited for their opinions. These potential referral resources need to know about your community. They are the influencers. They are the people you want to say "I've heard some excellent things about community XYZ." You need these people in your back pocket for their endorsements.

Positioning Your Community through Networking

How are these vital referral sources built? It is called networking and takes a sound plan that is well conceived and implemented. Like the marketing plan, the networking plan targets potential referral sources as part of a strategic outreach plan.

People who don't know about a community won't be able to refer it. Look at an under-performing community and consider the number and nature of meetings that the staff attends outside the community. Generally you will see a direct correlation between high vacancies and low outreach.

While some communities have a dedicated staff position allocated to outreach or community relations, others place this responsibility on the executive director/administrator or leasing staff. Still other communities may require everyone to commit to some type of outreach.

Most successful outreach programs need to be coordinated by the Leasing department, but it's important that those conducting the outreach be committed to this vital responsibility. A weak link doesn't effectively accomplish these goals.

Positioning your community effectively with outside networking means targeted individuals need to learn what you offer and what you are about. This strategy cannot be overused—network, network, and network, because receptiveness breeds success.

Primary and Secondary Influencers

Networking activities and organizations to be involved can be defined as targeting two key groups. The first of these are known as *primary influencers*—those who work with seniors on a regular basis. *Secondary influencers* are those people who may at some point be able to say they have heard of your community, but dealing with seniors is not their primary business.

An example would be a Chamber of Commerce expo. Those staffing a home healthcare service company's booth would be primary influencers. Chamber members in a variety of other businesses would be secondary influencers. They may have family members who could be potential residents and can help in spreading the word and telling your story.

All are worthwhile. It's a question of how much time and money you have at your disposal to cultivate them. Networking is the key to building anyone's business but effective networking means coming in contact with your customers and primary referral sources first.

Let's look at insurance salespeople for an example. They know that generally everyone will need insurance. Meanwhile, as effective networkers, they generously volunteer in as many ways as possible to be visible in the community and first build relationships of trust before soliciting appointments.

Networking gives you the opportunity to tell your story. There is still confusion about senior housing, and many families do not really know the differences among the housing options available and the types of care they offer. The perception that senior housing is "nursing home care" is still prevalent among adult children who have not had an opportunity to visit a senior community.

Building Your List

The first step toward building a list of networking resources is determining who comes into contact with seniors in your area and then strategizing how you will reach them. You have to determine who you need to meet first. Remember, they won't come to you; you have to go to them.

Potential sources include the following:
- Physician groups
- Hospitals
- Discharge planners
- Geriatric specialists and guardians
- Clergy
- Vendors (for example, medical supplies and orthopedic products)
- Senior organizations and senior centers
- Estate planning and trust attorneys
- CPAs
- Trust officers in banks
- Community organizations (Chambers, service clubs, women's groups)
- Groups geared to retired persons
- Competitive communities

You may want to become a member of some of these groups and there is occasionally overlap. Decide who on your staff will be assigned to an organization or is already a member. Try to integrate staff into the local community as much as possible to increase your exposure to networking possibilities. Matching staff interests to a specific group is helpful.

A successful owner-operator of a Virginia independent living community was not particularly involved in civic affairs. Nothing was going to make him sit at the Chamber luncheons when he felt he needed to be involved running the community. But he was active in his church. He volunteered for various committees and offered to hold upcoming monthly meetings using his community's dining room and food service. On this particular committee were prominent community leaders including several doctors and attorneys. In several months, referrals began to come from these fellow committee members as both they and their spouses knew more about the community.

You and your staff probably are more connected to the local community than you may initially realize. When someone attends a church, visits a health club, or visits his or her own physician, these are opportunities to help spread the word.

Networking is more than filling a chair at a Chamber breakfast. It involves proactively talking about the community in a positive light. For every table of ten where you sit, there are probably nine people who will be interested in your story. If you aren't prepared to tell your story, there may be someone else better suited for networking on behalf of the community.

Pounding the Pavement

The least popular type of networking is what we call *cold walking*—knocking on doors, dropping in, and leaving behind brochures and a gift.

How does a politician garner votes? Sometimes it's this tried and true technique of going door to door, but in a selective way. This same strategy can be applied to cold walking. Many times professionals are clustered in certain areas of town. One cold walking plan may involve assigning a staff member to take an afternoon and knock on these doors, dropping in to chat and leave behind a brochure. Pick out a professional medical building and start at the top floor, working your way down. Although many of us may cringe at the thought of cold walking, many warm to it once they have tried it. The results can be impressive.

Some people assume that if they visit an office once, the contact is made. But repetition is key. An effective networking plan should incorporate multiple visits. The first visit should always include obtaining the professional's business card and contact information, which is then input for the community's database.

Chapter 16:

Looking at Your Community from the Inside Out – It's All about the Customer

Always remember that no matter how much is spent on paid advertising, publicity, or events, the very best form of advertising is word of mouth. Whether passed on by residents themselves, families, friends, or professionals, the stories from satisfied residents are the most valuable type of referrals.

> When turning around an under-performing Florida community, there were a host of problems to solve. So few people were living there that very little was being spread by word of mouth, either by residents or families, whether good, bad, or indifferent. The community had many positives, but no one was creating any buzz. While a daughter of one of the residents felt very positive about the community, she told us she felt very guilty that her mother needed to live there rather than with the family. She found it awkward to extol positives about her mom's experience because she was admitting a failure within their family. That is a challenge to be tackled.

Although our focus is marketing rather than operations, the reality is that all aspects of a community affect residents' satisfaction which in turn impacts positive referrals for the community. From dining to transportation, activities to housekeeping, all become customer pluses or minuses depending upon residents' experiences. Unresolved customer service issues fester and eventually affect future leasing efforts.

At a troubled community we were repositioning, the young chef confided to me his feeling that residents didn't respect him or his staff. He said on one occasion he had snapped at a resident who was an incessant complainer about the temperature of the soup. While I tried to be sympathetic, what I saw was a young man who did not present a professional look. His chef's jacket was stained and unbuttoned, revealing a black t-shirt. He was wearing jeans, running shoes, and dark glasses. Not the right image. It was no surprise that residents were complaining; they didn't know how to criticize his appearance so they redirected their complaints to the staff about the food. Fortunately, the chef was replaced with a congenial fellow who enjoyed dressing the part of the profession. Food service complaints decreased as the white-cloaked chef wandered through the dining room during dinner or lunch.

A hands-on administrator should have required appropriate dress by the chef from the onset, but she was not seeing the situation from residents' vantage point. In her mind, she had a chef who was minding the kitchen, and food was served within budget.

Enduring Power of Superior Customer Service

Residents come first. They are, after all, the *raison d'etre* of the business. Remember that prospective residents don't wake up and jump for joy at the thought of moving to a senior community; they come with trepidation, expectations, specific needs, and a host of questions. Addressing these issues should always be priority number one for you and your staff.

Put yourself in the residents' shoes and mindset to be empathetic. For example, an interested prospect may ask about specific services your community provides and how to start the move-in process, but really want reassurance and someone to talk with who is a compassionate listener. If you can afford the luxury of a move-in coordinator, all the better. These coordinators can handle the myriad of details in a move, from making sure the phone line and electricity are connected to assisting on the day of the move—a traumatic event for many seniors who may not have family assistance.

One community prepared a move-in booklet that was given to prospects at the time of the contract signing. This included a step-by-step checklist and timetable for a move.

Another community stocks new residents' refrigerators with cold drinks, fruit, and sandwiches to help them feel at home that first day. It's a nice touch and one that impresses family members. If you have staff to help hang pictures and unpack boxes, terrific. If you can't provide such services, offer a list of companies specializing in these services.

Using resources familiar with your community is key. Understand that moving companies move things—they don't select appropriate furniture that will fit into an apartment. It's important to provide or recommend specialists in downsizing so excess furniture and home accessories are eliminated.

Welcoming New Residents

Make sure programs for integrating new residents into the community are well thought out. Moving to a community is much like the first day of school. This is a critical acclimating time. A warm, welcoming dining room manager who makes introductions and arranges for table companion can make all the difference in how quickly newcomers are integrated into the community. Do all you can to make those first few weeks as pleasant as possible.

One gentleman related that when the movers were unpacking, his electric razor was misplaced. The hospitality manager took matters in hand and found the missing item. This small touch made the new resident feel more comfortable. The manager also stayed on top of the cable company to assure his computer was connected. The resident never misses an opportunity to let the manager know of his appreciation; his family is grateful, as well.

In comparison, a gentleman living in a large, active adult condominium was unable to cook for himself after his wife died. He was subsisting on cans of tuna fish and cereal. He decided to move to a small, independent living community which offered a much improved lifestyle with meals, transportation, and companionship. Yet he paced the halls voicing his dissatisfaction with his new home. Finally the administrator spoke with his family, saying that if the gentleman was that unhappy he could return to the previous home without being obligated for the duration of the lease. When he moved out, an exit interview surfaced some vital information. He felt no one cared about him or made him feel welcomed. He sat in the dining room alone and no one took time to introduce him around. His departure showed that the community's failure to acclimate new residents meant his emotional needs were not being met.

A welcome packet for new residents should be created and include pertinent information about the community, from a summary of services (for example, dining room, beauty salon, and fitness center hours of operation) to a list of useful telephone numbers. Your new arrivals will be grateful and their families will thank you, too. Pattern the packet on a directory found in a hotel room if you need a template.

Directors of First Impressions and Incoming Telephone Calls

Good customer services extend to the seemingly simplest of issues like how telephone calls and messages are handled. Telephone mystery shopping often reveals how the community's first impressions are made, or not, by the person who answers the phone. Regardless of a community's size, there needs to be a plan in place to answer the telephone well, take messages, and transfer callers.

Someone calling to inquire about a community should need to call only once and should be treated as a high priority. No telephone should ring more than three times before being picked up. The plan should include how to handle calls received after hours and on holidays and weekends. Understandably you may not be able to staff 24/7, but those responsible for answering a telephone should be adequately trained in taking complete messages with names and call-back telephone numbers in a courteous and helpful manner. Plans also should be in place to transfer inquiries to managers on duty so interested parties have their questions answered.

Similarly if there are security guards at gatehouses, they need to be oriented to the community. They should be friendly greeters and helpful to visitors. If tours are scheduled, provide security guards with names of the day's planned visitors. That's a nice touch of hospitality.

Offering Directions to Help Customers Find You

Especially for older customers, trying to find your community may prove frustrating. Every front desk should have clear, printed directions that include all major roadways to your community. Any staff answering the front desk telephone should be briefed on providing verbal directions in a slow and polite way. Play the customer role and make sure visitors and prospects know how to find their way to your front door. GPS may be good, but some of us still get lost.

Once visitors arrive, what do they see? Are visitors' parking spaces designated and the front entrance clearly marked? Is there available parking? Is the paint peeling on the front door? Does the grass need cutting or is the shrubbery overdue for pruning? Try to see all of this through the fresh eyes of a prospective resident. Take corrective action where needed. First impressions are all-important.

Resident Requests

By anticipating requests in advance, assignments can be made to designated staff members. The worst-case response to a resident's request is "I'm not sure about that" or "That's impossible." It's important that residents are responded to quickly and problems are solved.

Disney Corporation and the Ritz Carlton Hotel chain have outstanding customer service programs for their employees that can be emulated by a senior housing community. Their creed is for each employee to take ownership for customer complaints and requests rather than passing them along to someone else. Staff is given responsibility for solving everyday problems. This type of training pays huge dividends.

Take special care to help residents feel they can maintain whatever activities they used to enjoy. From attending the city's Chamber of Commerce activities to shopping and volunteering, their lives should be enhanced. Make sure to always welcome family members. While holiday celebrations put pressure on staff due to an influx of families, these are important times. Arranging special activities for grandchildren and great-grandchildren demonstrates a caring attitude. One community's Sunday open house features sing-a-longs for all plus a clown and face-painting for little ones. Consideration for visiting grandchildren thrills the families of prospects.

...And More

Many communities do not have the luxury of a designated model apartment to show prospects. They use either a recently vacated apartment or willing residents' homes. In either case, these need to show appropriately. Soiled carpeting, odors, and broken or left-behind furniture do not project the image you want prospects to remember. "Someone just moved out" becomes a weak excuse. If you are using a resident's apartment, any visit needs to be planned in advance.

Providing appropriate assistance to surviving residents and family members when a resident passes on, or when they vacate for whatever reason, is important. Exit interviews reveal how dissatisfied families may be during crisis times when they quickly need to vacate an apartment. Plan in advance for assistance like providing boxes for packing and remembering a departed resident. This only adds to your reputation as a caring, professionally staffed community.

There are always going to be newer communities that are more luxurious or offer newer amenities. How do you compete? Superlative customer service can set you apart from the pack. This is how older communities survive amidst a wave of new communities. The well-established traditions of superior care and customer service become their hallmarks. Newer and bigger may in fact be impersonal when compared to the warmth and caring practiced by your community.

Chapter 17:

||||||||||||||||||||||||||||||||||||||||||||||||||||||||||||||||||||||||||||||||||||||||||||||||||||||||||

The Power of Relationships

Our customers are no different than the people in our families or ourselves. We all respond positively to someone remembering our name and smiling. A hug, handshake, or a light touch to our hand or arm gives us a warm feeling. I call this "power touch and listening" and these are critical selling skills. This is a prime reason that only key employees should be assigned to tour customers through a community rather than multiple employees or, in some cases, residents.

When a prospective customer makes a decision to research your community, it is so important first to create a relationship with the customer. Relationship-building skills require listening, and some employees may not have the gift of easily building rapport with customers and families. When someone tells me with pride that *all* employees tour visitors, I wonder if during a tour the chef must not be thinking of his kitchen responsibilities that he would rather address than patiently walking along with a customer.

In training rapport-building skills with sales and leasing teams, we find that it is more common to tour first then build rapport. A salesperson seems to find talking to prospects more comfortable while walking through the tour than engaging in discovery. But this scenario may occur: A family member walks in and asks the receptionist to see the two-bedroom apartments for her parents. The salesperson comes to the lobby with a brochure in hand and introduces herself. She proceeds to show the community to the visitor. This hypothetical daughter is approximately age 60. She follows the salesperson and sees the common rooms and a model. But the salesperson doesn't realize the daughter is only partially hearing what she is saying because they are walking and also because of a hearing deficit. There is a lot of information to retain as they tour and the experience is overwhelming to the daughter, who leaves frustrated and depressed.

In contrast, we recommend engaging in discovery *prior to* touring. A customer should be invited to a comfortable room and offered refreshments. Time is spent getting to know about the family. Open-ended questions like the following help get someone talking and elicit valuable information about the prospective resident:

- What are the customers' names?
- How does Mom (or how do you) spend the day?
- What does Dad (or what do you) enjoy doing?
- Tell me about their (or your) life?

A tour should be tailored to the interests and hobbies of the customer, so it's important to learn what those are. This way the salesperson can point out special community features that would appeal, such as a card room for an avid bridge player or a stocked library for a reader.

We are amazed to learn through telephone mystery shopping how few salespeople ask questions about families, from their names to how they are currently managing. Salespeople would much rather "data dump" a list of features and services and provide prices without any discovery about callers or their situation.

The Salesperson Holds the Key

Relationships take time, and nurturing them may seem counter to a salesperson's desire for move-ins. The ability to connect with the family is especially critical; it not only creates a successful climate for the resident, it also nurtures customer satisfaction and future referrals down the road. From inviting prospects and families to lunch or dinner to visiting someone in his or her home, successful salespeople are learning they need to go the extra yard to close deals. Their competitors will be doing this if they are not.

We encourage creativity. Today's salesperson should have a "bucket" of strategies to pull from to create a trusting relationship with the prospect. They need to be empowered to do things like send cards and flowers on special days, write personal notes, and give books or a costume jewelry pin. Any of these tactics may be well worth the effort and affect closing ratios.

Salespeople need to be encouraged to visit the customer in his or her home, if necessary (certainly not in lieu of a first visit to the community, but if the customer has specific needs that could be addressed by a home visit). We knew of a customer who was living alone on a farm after her husband died and wanted to move to a community, but it wasn't until two salespeople visited could they understand her obstacle. The farm house was chock-a-block full and she didn't know where to start downsizing.

A successful salesperson needs to excel in the ability to empathize with each customer. Each person's needs and motivations are somewhat different, and the key is listening with heart as well as one's head.

Believe and the Customer Will Believe

Successful salespeople believe in their heart that someone's life will be better if they move to the community they represent. We have found salespeople who become robotic in their presentations and tend to talk features rather than benefits, which may leave prospects cold.

Touch: A Basic Need

When you are working with senior clients, the reassurance of a pat on the hand or a light hug can be a miracle worker if it is heartfelt and appropriate. While some of us are not "touchy" people (I would find it awkward to put my arm around a stranger), any of us can grasp someone's hand as in a greeting. According to findings from the University of Miami's School of Medicine, the Touch Research Institute, "Touch is a basic physiological need. What we've found out in studies of the elderly population is that people who are touched get sick less often. They have fewer visits to the doctor's office. They become more social and develop healthier habits."

I interviewed a salesperson once who asked, if we hired him, would we have a problem finding him playing pool in the afternoon with a prospect. This was one of his techniques to build rapport with his prospects. I asked how he would build similar rapport with female prospects who may prefer bridge to pool. But his heart was in the right place and I appreciated his warmth and interest in his clients.

A continuing care community with which I'm familiar is well known for hosting an annual seafood dinner for waiting-list future residents and qualified prospects. An invitation to this event has become quite coveted. The director of sales spends considerable time on seating charts, putting together people from the same geographic areas, who attended the same college, or who served in the same branch of the military. This takes some discovery with his prospects. He greets everyone warmly and there are plenty of hugs. This director of sales has learned how to build relationships with his customers. He becomes a surrogate son. His efforts pay off in healthy sales ratios and yearly bonus.

Body Language Talks, Too

In the book *Body Language* by Julius Fast, the author makes the point that body language and spoken language are interdependent. If we listen only to the words when someone is talking, we may get as much of a distortion as we would if we listened only to the body language. Pay attention to both the body language and the words that are spoken. Showing empathy through your body language is important, too. If you are taller than a prospect, it is often helpful to suggest you both occasionally sit during the tour to help the prospect feel at ease.

Good listening can be facilitated by thoughtful seating arrangements. A traditional desk and visitor chair configuration may be comfortable, but a round table with chairs or living room-style lounge chairs may be useful alternatives.

Some customers may be needing reassurance. Although they may not be able to verbalize this, it can be read in their body language. Here again, discovery and bonding with customers may reveal their concerns. Ask questions about family and life experiences, show that you are sincerely interested, and give complete eye contact and attention. A salesperson, when touring, gazed out an apartment's window and a mystery shopper interpreted this as being disinterested. This small gesture was very significant as they lost some of the momentum of a tour. This could have been avoided with careful body language.

Chapter 18:

||||||||||||||||||||||||||||||||||||||||||||||||||||||||||||||||||||||||||||||||||||||||||||||||||||

How Are We Doing? –
Monitoring and Measuring Marketing Efforts

As marketing professionals, we are often frustrated at not being able to match effort and money expended with the results achieved. There is no way around it; marketing is not an exact science. And the most frustrating aspect of the business is no matter how many move-in's there are today, there are apartments being vacated at the same time by the back-door effect.

Success can be multi-pronged. It can be measured by the amount of traffic produced by an ad, the attendance at an event, the number of inquiries per day, or the number of people who walk through the door who just happened to be driving by.

> A developer with whom we worked would call the leasing office every Sunday for the week's total number of leases signed. He was not interested in tours, traffic, or that the recent open house had record-setting attendance. He didn't want to hear about the compliments received. He wanted only the results. We would try to explain that the decision to move to a community was a process that would take several months; it was very positive that a prospect had returned with her family to take another look at an apartment. But the developer felt only signed leases truly measured success.

> We once partnered with an advertising agency that always believed any results were generated from ads. While efforts were made with any number of strategies such as direct mail, publicity, and salespeople making follow-up telephone calls—or a combination of all these tactics—the agency insisted it was the ad that achieved the results. And the bigger the ad, the better—because everyone would be sure to see it.

Measuring marketing success takes time collecting data to establish benchmarks. Collecting data and entering it in computer programs for easy tracking provides a history for later reference. It helps to use a registration form for inquiries. Historical information to be gathered would include:

- How did the prospect hear of the community?
- What is the zip code/address of the prospect?
- Does the prospect rent or own a home/apartment?
- What is the projected timetable of the prospect?

It is also important to know what marketing action triggered the inquiry, as well as if it resulted in a sale and the length of time involved. Over time, accumulated data can be analyzed for trends indicating what methods consistently create traffic.

Figure 18-1. Sample prospect registration form.			
Last name:			(Jr., III):
First name – 1:	First name – 2:		Title (Mr., Mrs., Dr.):
Address – 1:		Address – 2:	
City:	State:	Zip:	Phone:
2 – Party lead: Y / N	Prospective resident: Y / N Other Party: Prospective res. In system: Y / N Relationship:		

Age – 1:	Age – 2:	Marital status:	Entry code:	
Contact type:	Contact result:	Apt. type:	Status code:	Hot button:
Salesperson:		Initial date of lead:	Follow-up date:	
Comments:				

Keeping Track

There are software programs specialized in the senior housing industry that are easy to use to manage leads and data. Other contact management programs can be adapted for smaller communities. In either case, it is important to record data that extends beyond a name and address and to use software rather than a box of index cards. Cards can be misplaced and are cumbersome to tally and work with. Should employees be terminated, a box of valuable leads can mysteriously disappear.

Today's employees need to be computer literate and receptive to using the programs for the industry. "Garbage in…garbage out" applies to any database, so it should be reviewed periodically for accuracy and to make sure staff is correctly inputting data.

What works in one geographic market may not work as well in another location, but it's possible to identify helpful trends. For example, you can see whether monthly open houses create noticeable qualified traffic or simply traffic, or if telephone inquiries increase when ads appear in a specific publication. Are people using the Yellow Pages or are they using a web site? Did an article generate traffic?

Keep in mind that in new communities, when first building name awareness, there may not be a huge conversion of inquiries to sales or deposits. In the early stages of the leasing cycle, it takes time to build trust and momentum.

When we were advertising a new community on the Gulf coast of Florida, several full-page ads did not produce a significant number of calls in relationship to their costs. When we switched to smaller ads and increased the frequency, we found telephone inquiries increased. And when advertising was coupled with promotional events, the results significantly improved. Lesson learned: there are no hard and fast rules. Alternatives needed to be carefully tested in specific geographic areas. What had worked on the east coast of Florida was not a technique embraced by the west coast's population. Larger was not better. Also by reading the paper daily we found we were competing with three other new communities that were opening at the same time.

Gauging Direct Mail Success

To measure success of a direct mail program, you will want to know what the direct mail effort was, the response mechanism (coupon, offer, telephone call, and so on), the location of respondents, zip code analysis, and the cost of the mailing list.

The term "call to action" means how the customer responds to whatever is being mailed. If you want to test the effectiveness of a particular promotional piece, try running a special offer with the piece. Code the response coupons as well as any reply cards and then check the results. If prospects call with inquiries, try to find if they are responding to the direct mail item or if they were motivated by another advertising technique.

Telemarketing Surveys

It may be of value to use telemarketing surveys to purge or refresh a database that has been built over time. These surveys can assess quality of leads and check to see if responses garnered by a telemarketer match those compiled by sales staff.

While every salesperson may make calls each day, there simply is a limit to the number of calls that physically can be made by staff. Telemarketing can be useful to place additional calls. Although this can be handled by phone rooms and computerized call machines, the senior customer responds much better to individual phone calls made by a person who is specialized in dealing with seniors. They may or may not be associated with your company; this can be outsourced to specialists. A script can be created that is sensitive to the customer and designed to elicit data that can be updated in the lead database.

Resident Satisfaction Surveys

Residents and families may offer constructive information via resident satisfaction surveys. These can be undertaken yearly to gauge resident reaction to services being provided, staff, and any number of issues. Soliciting feedback is vital to resident retention, but residents need to see improvements as a result of a survey.

Recognize that relying only on surveys may not provide a complete picture, and community audits by outside consultants are useful, as well.

Don't Stop Marketing

Even if you are 100 percent occupied and have a waiting list, the biggest mistake you can make is to stop marketing. The analogy to a water faucet is appropriate. If the faucet is turned off, the momentum is not sustained. Marketing needs consistency. From advertising to outreach, there needs to be continual efforts directed to marketing since we never can close the back door in the senior housing business.

As communities mature, we continually find it is resident word of mouth that drives traffic. But seeing captivating advertising and reading about the community can spark the word-of-mouth momentum. It takes a concerted effort of cohesive marketing to continue to bring traffic to the door.

We once were working with a community whose management announced they were slashing our advertising budget for the year when apartments were filled. Within six months, they found how wrong they were. The innovative marketing programs used initially for lease-up needed to be quickly reinstated. Far more dollars were expended to restart the marketing engines than would have been spent to keep them running.

On the flip side, there is sometimes the urge to spend money for new ads when, in essence, ads have greater longevity than believed. The desire for a new campaign might stem from a salesperson who feels the current ads aren't working when, in reality, what is missing is simply the willingness to make necessary sales follow-up calls.

Communication Audits

If you want to know what a cross-section of people think about your community, consider a communications audit. This can let you know if your marketing approach is effective and how well your brand is perceived.

A community in which we conducted a communications audit was an excellent community and had held promotional events and direct mail. The audit revealed they were missing reaching their target audiences and, in many cases, were the best-kept secret in town. The communications audit included personal interviews with influencers in the city where the community was located and provided insights to correct the advertising messaging. Another benefit of the audit was in soliciting insights; information about the community was disseminated to key influencers to help in spreading the word. The result: a win-win for marketing.

Focus Groups

By bringing together a group of residents or prospective residents with an unbiased facilitator, much can be gleaned about your community. As you might expect, the presence of owners, administrators, and staff tends to bias the group. In their absence, residents feel more comfortable to let you know about the community from their vantage point. Be forewarned that usually they don't hold back.

Sitting with one such group of residents, it was easy to learn that they loved the community's staff but felt the community was skimping on food costs with a monotonous menu. They said that while the chef's presentations for parties were impressive, the daily dinner entrees lacked imagination and variety.

Focus groups can be full scale with two-way mirrors and recorded sessions or they can be informal. We use an informal style to bring residents together with our creative teams from interior designers to copywriters and graphic artists. Often images of why people move to a senior community quickly change once someone hears first hand and is involved one-on-one with residents. If you want to infuse some "ground-truthing" and new excitement into your ads, collateral, and Internet communicating, try this technique.

Exit Interviews

Families of residents often provide valuable insights after their family member has vacated a community. The truth may not be fully told to an employee but with a trained listener, worthwhile constructive information can be learned through exit interviews. This is a low-cost method and helpful in continuing good relationships with families. No more than five questions should be asked by the caller and there should be ample time to listen to someone's positive and negative comments.

Marketing Audits

It is important to view your community as would a customer visiting for the first time. Marketing audits evaluate these first impressions and can also delve deeper into a total critique of all aspects of marketing for a community. It is important to learn how a community is perceived and where there are strengths and weaknesses.

We find many issues that easily can be corrected or improved to make a better first and lasting impression. From time lags responding to Internet requests, to model apartments that were used as guest suites and then not readied to show, marketing audits take all aspects into account while also analyzing database entries and lead source analysis.

Conclusion

Senior housing marketing is dynamic, fast-changing, and challenging. Successful marketing takes careful planning and budgeting, a sensitivity to the customer's needs and situation, and effective use of all the tools of the trade. This is a relationship business and requires a caring and personal approach to meet the changing expectations of seniors.

Your work is cut out for you. In the years ahead, we will continue to see dramatic changes to the senior housing industry as the Boomer population matures and retires. The marketing strategies and techniques described in the book have served me well. I sincerely hope they will guide you to your own path of success.

CPSIA information can be obtained at www.ICGtesting.com
Printed in the USA
BVOW04s1227150415

396289BV00001B/114/P